KĀLIDĀSA

About the Author

Professor Ram Gopal, the author of the present book, is now Kalidasa Professor of Sanskrit and Head, Department of Kalidasa Chair. Panjab University, Chandigarh. He is an eminent Sanskrit scholar of international repute whose numerous research publications including *India of Vedic Kalpasūtras, Vaidika Vyākaraṇa* (in two volumes); *Vaidika Vyākhyā-Vivechana; The History and Principles of Vedic Interpretation; Vedic Thought and Its Influence on Indian Culture; The Veda and the Mahābhārata; The Veda and the Bhagavad- gītā; The Historicity of the Mahābhārata War; Westward Migration of Indian Stories*; and *The Secular Origin of Sanskrit Drama* have won world-wide fame. In recognition of his outstanding contributions to the realm of Sanskrit studies he was awarded the Independence Day Award, *Certificate of Honour in Sanskrit,* by the President of India in 1971; and in the same year he was honoured by the Haryana Government also with the States' Highest Literary Award in Sanskrit and a Felicitation Volume. The Ministry of Education and Culture, Government of India, honoured him in 1981 with a Literary Award of Rs. 10,000 in appreciation of his reputed research publication *Vaidika Vyākaraṇa* (in two volumes) which was selected by the University Grants Commisson for this prestigious Award.

KĀLIDĀSA

His Art and Culture

By

Ram Gopal, M.A., Ph. D.

Certificate of Honour in Sanskrit,
Kalidasa Professor of Sanskrit and Head,
Department of Kalidasa Chair,
Panjab University, Chandigarh.

CONCEPT PUBLISHING COMPANY PVT. LTD.
NEW DELHI-110059

ISBN: 978-81-7022-145-6

First Published 1984

Published and Printed by

Concept
Since 1974

Concept Publishing Company Pvt. Ltd.
A/15-16, Commercial Block, Mohan Garden,
New Delhi-110059 (India)
T : 91-11-41101460
E : publishing@conceptpub.com, *W*: www.conceptpub.com

To
My Wife
Shrimati Sushila Devi

क्रियाणां खलु धर्म्याणां सत्पत्न्यो मूलकारणम् ।

"Virtuous wives are indeed mainly instrumental in the performance of religious duties."

Kālidāsa

PREFACE

Kālidāsa is a name to conjure with not only in Indian literature but also in world literature. His plays, epics and lyrics which represent the acme of Sanskrit literature have exercised great influence on the later Indian literature and won the admiration and appreciation of ancient Indian literary critics as well as modern connoisseurs.

In the last quarter of the eighteenth century when some Western scholars began to evince interest in Sanskrit literature, Kālidāsa topped the list of Sanskrit authors whose works caught the fancy of the pioneers of Sanskrit studies in the West. So the first Sanskrit play to be translated in any European language was Kālidāsa's masterpiece, *Abhijñānaśākuntala*, the first English translation of which was brought out by Sir William Jones in the year 1789. Besides, the same scholar published in 1792 the first edition of Kālidāsa's lyric poem *Ṛtusaṃhāra.* The said English version of the *Abhijñānaśākuntala* was rendered into German by Georg Forster in 1791. It was this German translation of Kālidāsa's famous play which evoked the applause of such eminent German connoisseurs as Goethe and Herder. Goethe's epigram in praise of the *Abhijñānaśākuntala* has been cited by us in Chapter I (p. 1) of the present work. Herder's enthusiastic appreciation of the *Śākuntala* may be gauged from the following paragraph of his letter addressed to a friend : "Do you not wish with me that, instead of these endless religious books of the Vedas, Upavedas and Upāṅgas, they would give us the more useful and more agreeable works of the Indians, and especially their poetry of every kind ? It is here that the mind and character of a nation is best brought to life before us, and I gladly admit that I have got a more accurate and more real notion of the manner of thinking of ancient Indians from this *Śakuntalā* (*Abhijñānaśākuntala*) than from all their Upnekats (*Upaniṣads*) and Bagavedams

(*Bhāgavatapurāṇa*)." (*Herder's Schriften*, vol. IX, p. 226, Zur schönen Literatur und Kunst, Tübingen, 1807 ; Cf. Max Müller's *History of Ancient Sanskrit Literature*, 1968 reprint, pp. 4-5). Although Herder was not in a position to form a correct idea of the contents and significance of the religious books of ancient India owing to the lack of their standard translations in German, his lavish praise of this famous Sanskrit play is particularly noteworthy.

In the course of the last two hundred years the works of Kālidāsa have been edited many a time with several Sanskrit commentaries, translated into numerous languages of the world with copious annotations, and subjected to a variety of literary, critical and historical studies by so many eminent scholars in India and abroad. A comprehensive work containing a sifting review of all the modern studies devoted to Kālidāsa is still a desideratum. It would undoubtedly require a very large volume to give an up-to-date, analytical, complete and critical account of all types of modern studies on Kālidāsa ; and it is beyond the scope of our present work to attempt such a stupendous task. However, some of the outstanding studies on various aspects of Kālidāsa's works have been listed by us in the *Select Bibliography* appended to the present work. Since a comprehensive review of all sorts of opinions expressed during the last two hundred years on the life, works and date of Kālidāsa falls outside the purview of the present work, in the First and Second Chapter of this work we have referred to only important views of eminent writers on the subject. The principal aim of the present work is two-fold :

(*i*) to dispel some current confusion and misconceptions about the various aspects of Kālidāsa's life, works, date and thought ; and

(*ii*) to present succinctly a clear, correct and rational account of his art and culture on the basis of an intensive study of the original sources in the light of modern researches so that even a layman may be able to appreciate properly the literary excellence and cultural refinement of Kālidāsa who has been acclaimed by Sir Monier-Williams as 'the Shakespeare of India.'

In the absence of an analytical and critical appraisal of the important theories advanced hitherto on various aspects of Kālidāsa's life, works and date, the multiplicity of divergent and contradictory views on the subject is likely to confuse an average reader about the position and attainments of our most celebrated poet-playwright. For instance, the divergent interpretations put on certain striking similarities of ideas and expression between the works of Kālidāsa and Aśvaghoṣa have led to the formulation of two contradictory theories on the relationship between these two illustrious authors. Since 1893, when Aśvaghoṣa's epic poem *Buddhacharita* was first published by E.B. Cowell from Oxford, most of the Western scholars have been advocating Aśvoghoṣa's priority to Kālidāsa on the assumption that the latter has imitated the ideas and expression of the former. But several Indian scholars have controverted this hypothesis and expressed the opposite view. Thus there is a good deal of confusion among students of Kālidāsa on this point as well as on many other aspects of his life, works, ideas and ideals. We have, therefore, endeavoured in the present work to dispel some current misconceptions about Kālidāsa and to give an accurate account of his art and culture as revealed in his works. In keeping with Mallinātha's well known dictum *nāmūlam likhyate kiñchin nānapekṣitam uchyate*, all our conclusions are supported by quotations from or references to the original sources. A fairly large number of Sanskrit verses, shedding welcome light on various important aspects of the art and culture of Kālidāsa, have been cited and translated by us in the present work. It has been our constant endeavour to convey in translation the sense of the original verses as accurately as possible in consonance with the Sanskrit usage and context ; and we have therefore refrained from giving a punctiliously literal rendering of the Sanskrit stanzas. Although some modern scholars have attempted a metrical translation of Sanskrit verses, we are not in favour of a metrical translation and in this regard we are inclined to concur with F. Max Müller who observes "that a metrical translation is often an excuse only for an inaccurate translation" (*Sacred Books of the East*, Vol. 32, Introduction, p. x). Moreover, the rhythm and charm of a Sanskrit metre, which can be enjoyed in its original verse only, cannot be fully represented in a metrical translation.

Therefore, a metrical translation is more often than not a misrepresentation of an original Sanskrit verse.

No authentic biography of Kālidāsa is available at present, and the anecdota contained in some later works about his life are apocryphal and worthless as discussed by us in Chapter 1. Similarly the attempts of some modern scholars to pinpoint his birth-place are equally unsuccessful, in spite of his marked predilection for Ujjayinī. Kālidāsa's broad national outlook is amply reflected in his works as shown by us in this Chapter.

Chapter 2 which deals with the problem of fixing the date of Kālidāsa examines in depth the chronological relationship between Kālidāsa and Aśvaghoṣa in the light of numerous verbatim agreements between the works of these two authors. It is important to note in this connection that Aśvaghoṣa's two epic poems, viz., *Buddhacharita* and *Saundarananda*, betray so many verbatim agreements not only with the works of Kālidāsa but also with several other works of earlier Sanskrit literature, such as the *Rāmāyaṇa*, the *Mahābhārata*, the *Upaniṣads* and *Bhāsa's* play *Pratijñā-Yaugandharāyaṇa*, as discussed by us in this Chapter. Since it seems to be utterly inconceivable that besides Bhāsa and Kālidāsa the authors of the *Upaniṣads*, the *Rāmāyaṇa* and the *Mahābhārata* borrowed verbatim passages and phrases from the works of Aśvaghoṣa, the obvious inference is that it is Aśvaghoṣa who resorts to verbatim borrowing from the works of his illustrious predecessors including Bhāsa and Kālidāsa with a view to enhancing the effectiveness of his (Aśvaghoṣa's) poems which are avowedly composed by him to preach Buddhistic teachings and not for aesthetic pleasure. Aśvaghoṣa's blatant verbatim borrowing from the works of Kālidāsa, as shown by us in the present work, points to the conclusion that the latter must have flourished at least a century earlier than the former. This literary evidence coupled with some other important pieces of chronological evidence leads us to the inference that Kālidāsa who is definitely anterior to Aśvaghoṣa may be tentatively placed between 50 B.C. and 50 A.D.

Kālidāsa's poetic art, as discussed by us in Chapter 3, is marked by polish and perfection and serves as a beacon to the later poets. His poetic art is noted for elegance, accomplishment, and harmony of sound and sense. His charming and thought-provoking poetry reveals his keen observation of Nature and penetrating insight into human sentiments. Kālidāsa who is universally acclaimed as a poet of beauty, harmony and perfection creates enchanting word-pictures and expresses human feelings with poise and restraint. In his flight of imagination he conceives of only beautiful, pleasant, delightful and harmonious aspects of life and Nature. His polished, perfect, charming and inspiring poetry delights our heart and elevates our soul. The study of Sanskrit literature is incomplete without a study of Kālidāsa's immortal lyrics, epics and plays.

Kālidāsa who is styled by Sir Monier-Williams as the Shakespeare of India ranks foremost among the best dramatists of the world. A gradual development is clearly discernible in Kālidāsa's dramatic art, as discussed by us in Chapter 4. His dramatic art reaches its zenith in his masterpiece, *Abhijñānaśākuntala*, which amply demonstrates the ingenuity of his creative genius and the perfection of his art in the construction of the plot, in sharp characterisation, in the unique delineation of love and pathos, in the sympathetic treatment of Nature, in poetic justice, in the elegance and felicity of expression, in the fusion of sound and sense, and in a wonderful blend of natural and supernatural elements. Enthralled by such rare and superb qualities of this play the famous German poet Goethe eulogistically describes it as combining heaven and earth and offering the blossoms of youth and the fruits of maturity, charms and delights, and satisfaction and support.

Kālidāsa's language, as discussed by us in Chapter 5, is simple, clear and free from long compounds and bombastic words. He skilfully chooses simple words of standard usage to construct significant and suggestive sentences and catchy phrases. His works present the best specimen of the *Vaidarbha* style of composition which is characterised by the commendable qualities of clarity, alegence, felicity, employment of metaphorical expression, and avoidance of harsh sounds and long compounds. Kālidāsa has complete command of the Sanskrit language and displays his perfect mastery of its nuances and subtleties. He employs over two dozen metres in his works and varies the metres of his verses to conform to the nature of description. A large number of figures of speech are aptly employed in his works. The imagery of Kālidāsa reveales his power of imagination, refinement of thought, outlook on life, keen observation of Nature, and mastery of various branches of knowledge. The selected Sanskrit verses, exemplifying various figures of speech in the present work, afford us an insight into Kālidāsa's sagacity and culture.

Kālidāsa's fascinating, inimitable and imaginative description of Nature, as discussed by us in Chapter 6, adds charm and beauty to his poetry and reveals his broad vision. Casual readers sometimes misunderstand Kālidāsa's concept of beauty and love and overlook the basic fact that in spite of sensuous description of beauty in his works he disapproves of sensuality and propounds the lofty ideal of pure, sincere and lasting conjugal love, as discussed by us in the concluding Chapter of this work. It may be particularly pointed out in this connection that Kālidāsa does not confine his view to skin-deep beauty and lays great strees on noble and spiritual qualities of character. His charming art is tempered with the ideals of balanced life set forth in the holy scriptures. It is no exaggeration to state that Kālidāsa's plays and poems not only represent the best models of *belles-lettres* but also convey in a subtle and charming manner the eternal message of moral virtues. In short, the works of Kālidāsa present a unique blend of fine art, refined culture, religious fervour and elevating thought.

In conclusion I wish to express my gratitude to all those scholars whose Sanskrit commentaries, books or articles on Kālidāsa have been consulted by me. My cordial thanks are due to my esteemed and learned friend, Professor Jagan Nath Agrawal, who generously spared his precious time to discuss with me some knotty problems concerning Kālidāsa and to offer some useful suggestions.

Department of Kālidāsa Chair,
Panjab University,
CHANDIGARH

RAM GOPAL

November 17, 1983.

CONTENTS

LIST OF ABBREVIATIONS

B	=	Buddhacharita
Bh. G	=	Bhagavadgītā
I.H.Q.	=	Indian Historical Quarterly
KS.	=	Kumārasambhava
Māl.	=	Mālavikāgnimitra
Mbh.	=	Mahābhārata
Megh.	=	Meghadūta
R.	=	Rāmāyaṇa of Vālmīki
Ragh.	=	Raghuvaṃśa
RS.	=	Ṛtusaṃhāra
RV.	=	Ṛgveda
Śak.	=	Abhijñānaśākuntala (Śākuntala)
S.	=	Saundarananda
Vik.	=	Vikramorvaśīya

1

The Life and Works of Kālidāsa

Kālidāsa, the immortal poet and playwright, is a peerless genius whose works have won world-wide fame. The matchless qualities of his works have been lavishly praised both by the ancient Indian critics and modern scholars. Daṇḍin and Bāṇa, two famous prose-writers of Sanskrit, pay rich tributes to Kālidāsa. Daṇḍin[1] compliments Kālidāsa on polishing the *Vaidarbha* style of composition and Kālidāsa's sweet and charming sayings are lauded in Bāṇa's *Harṣacharita*.[2] The names of Rājaśekhara, Śrīkṛṣṇakavi, Padmagupta, Soḍhala and Govardhanāchārya figure prominently among the eminent ancient admirers of Kālidāsa. Several ancient Indian legends concerning Kālidāsa testify to his unparalleled popularity since early times.

In modern times the translations of Kālidāsa's works in numerous Indian and foreign languages have spread his fame all over the world and now he ranks among the few topmost poets and playwrights of the world. It was only a German translation of Kālidāsa's famous play *Abhijñāna-Śākuntala* (popularly known as *Śakuntalā* after the name of its heroine), based on its English translation by William Jones, which impressed the renowned German poet Goethe to such an extent that he composed a verse in German to extol this wonderful drama.[3] Goethe's epigram may be translated as follows :

Wouldst thou have the blossoms of youth
    and the fruits of maturity,
Wouldst thou have charms and delights,
Wouldst thou have satisfaction and support,
Wouldst thou grasp the heaven and the earth
    with a single name,

I name thee, O Śakuntalā!
and thus everything is said.

Nearer home the celebrated poet Rabindranath Tagore not only propagated Kālidāsa's works and expounded their meaning and philosophy but also wrote a poem in Bengali in praise of the immortal poet-dramatist. An English rendering[4] of the last stanza of the poem is reproduced below :

Did you not have joy and sorrow,
Hope and despair, even like ourselves,
O immortal poet? Were not there always
The intrigues of a royal court, the stabbing in the back?
Did you never suffer humiliation,
Affront, distrust, injustice,
Want, hard and pitiless? Did you never pass
A sleepless night of poignant agony?
Yet above them all, unconcerned pure,
Has flowered your poem—a lotus of beauty
Opening to the sun of joy. Nowhere
Does it show any sign of sorrow, affliction, evil times.
Churning the sea of life you drank the poison,
The nectar that arose you gave away!

No authentic information is available about the life and date of the immortal poet-playwright who has left an indelible imprint on the later Indian mind. In fact his unparalleled popularity led to the invention of several stories about his life and character. According to one such story, Kālidāsa who was originally an illiterate idiot was fraudulently married to a princess and was thrown out by her on discovering his ignorance; and later he acquired extraordinary intelligence and erudition through the grace of the goddess Kālī whence he got the name Kālidāsa, i.e., a slave of Kālī. It is further narrated in the story that when Kālidāsa returned to his wife after attaining deep learning she asked him : *asti kaśchid vāgviśeṣaḥ* (Is there any excellence in your speech?). In response to this query Kālidāsa composed his three famous works—the *Kumārasambhava* opening with the word *asti*, the *Meghadūta* with the word *kaśchit* and the *Raghuvaṁśa* with the word *vāk*.

According to another apocryphal story, Kālidāsa was murdered by a greedy courtesan during his sojourn in Ceylon as a guest of his friend and Ceylonese King Kumāradāsa, because she desired to pass off before the King as her own composition the complementary part, *Bāle tava mukhāmbhoje katham indīvara-dvayam* (O Maiden, how are there two blue lotuses on your face-lotus), of the enigmatic verse : *kamale kamalotpattiḥ śrūyate na tu dṛśyate* (The growth of a lotus on a lotus is only heard but never seen).

No credence can similarly be given to another story which says that Kālidāsa was a court-poet of King Bhoja of Dhārā who flourished in the eleventh Century A.D. A statement contained in a late work entitled *Jyotirvidābharaṇa* erroneously ascribed to Kālidāsa counts Kālidāsa among the nine gems of the court of King Vikramāditya who vanquished the Śakas. There is a lot of controversy about the identification of Vikramāditya Śakāri, and it is an anachronism to regard some of the eminent court-gems like Vararuci and Varāhamihira as contemporaries.

Several modern scholars including my revered Guru, the late Mahāmahopādhyāya Dr. Lachhmi Dhar Kalla,[5] have put forward divergent views about the birth-place of Kālidāsa. Dr. Kalla has propounded the thesis that Kālidāsa's minute and graphic description of the Himālayas betrays his close acquaintance with the topography of Kashmir; that several rivers, hills, hermitages and holy places described in Kālidāsa's works are situated in Kashmir; that marriage rites and customs described by the poet are prevalent in Kashmir; that the Kashmirian Śaiva doctrine of *pratyabhijñāna-darśana* (the doctrine of the recognition of the unity of the divine soul) is adumbrated in the plays of Kālidāsa; and that the description of the saffron plant in the *Raghuvaṁśa* together with the preceding pieces of evidence points to the conclusion that Kālidāsa was born and brought up in Kashmir, although he later migrated to Central India to seek royal patronage due to disturbed conditions in Kashmir.

Explaining his name *Kālidāsa* as a devotee of the goddess Kālī, some scholars assign his birth-place to Bengāl on account of the predominance of the worship of Kālī in Bengāl. But it is a very weak argument, because the internal evidence available from Kālidāsa's works does not corroborate the view that he was a devotee of Kālī.[6] Moreover, it has to be borne in mind that the worship of Kālī (alias Kālikā or Durgā or *Chaṇḍī*) has been prevalent in the Himālayas and the adjoining areas since early times. For instance, the Mahābhārata[7] mentions a *tīrtha* named *Kālikāśrama* on the bank of the river Beas in Punjāb. Besides, Vyāsa's mother Satyavatī is known as *Kālī* also in the Great Epic.

Similarly Kālidāsa's fondness for *Vaidarbha* style of composition is taken as a basis by some scholars for assigning his birth-place to Vidarbha; and support for this argument is sought in Kālidāsa's references to Vidarbha in his works a few times. But no argument about the birth-place of a writer can be built on the basis of his style of writing.

It cannot be gainsaid that Kālidāsa had a great liking for Ujjayinī and the river Śiprā flowing by it. In his *Meghadūta* he devotes nearly a dozen stanzas to the warm description of the beautiful ladies, palatial buildings, glittering bazaars and salubrious surroundings of his favourite city which he fondly describes as a resplendent fragment of heaven (*infra*, Chapter III). Besides, Kālidāsa in his *Meghadūta* betrays his close acquaintance with several other places, rivers and hills situated in Central India, e g., the *Daśārṇa* country with its capital city named *Vidiśā*, *Daśapura* (Mandasor), the rivers *Revā*, *Vetravatī*, *Charmaṇvatī*, *Vananadī*, *Nirvindhyā* and *Gambhīrā* and the hills *Nīchairgiri* and *Devagiri* (*infra*, Chapter III). Kālidāsa's deep attachment to Ujjayinī coupled with his intimate knowledge of the geography of this region suggests that he spent the best part of his life in this city, whatever might have been his birth-place.

However, it must be pointed out at the same time that Kālidāsa,who had widely travelled throughout the length and breadth of India and had fully imbibed our ancient Indian culture, was a truly national poet with a broad outlook as attested by his writings. In his *Meghadūta* Kālidāsa requests the cloud-messenger to proceed from *Daśapura* to the famous battlefield of *Kurukṣetra* in the *Brahmāvarta* country and to enjoy the sacred waters of the river Sarasvatī. Then the cloud is requested to go to his destination *Alakā* on Mount *Kailāsa* via the vicinity of *Kanakhala*[8] where the river Gaṅgā descends from the

Himālayas. In the Fourth Canto of the *Raghuvaṁśa* where Raghu's conquest in all directions is described Kālidāsa displays his intimate knowledge of mountains, forests, rivers, towns, notable products, fashions and customs of various parts of India. For instance, there he speaks of the betel and the fermented coco-drink of *Kaliṅga*, of the pearl fisheries near the mouth of the river *Tāmraparṇī*, of the sandal forests of the *Malaya* and *Dardura* mountains, of the hair-fashion of the ladies of *Kerala*, of the beards of the Persians looking like beehives, of the saffron plant of Kashmir (or Bactria, see Note 12 of Chapter II), and of the black fragrant Aloe trees (*Kālāguru*) of *Prāg-Jyotiṣa* in the extreme east (*infra*, Chapter III). Besides, Kālidāsa describes in his works the Himālayas, the Vindhyas, the Indian Ocean and several rivers, lakes, forests and natural scenery of various parts of India (*infra*, Chapter VI).

Although a large number of Sanskrit works are traditionally attributed to Kālidāsa, most of the modern scholars are of the opinion that only two epics (*Mahākāvyas*), namely, the *Raghuvaṁśa* and the *Kumārasambhava*, two lyrics (*Khaṇḍakāvyas*) named *Ṛtusaṁhāra* and *Meghadūta*, and three plays, viz., the *Mālavikāgnimitra*, the *Vikramorvaśīya* and the *Abhijñāna-Śākuntala*, can be legitimately ascribed to him on the grounds of common ideas, expressions and style. There is a good deal of controversy about the chronological sequence of these seven works. So far as the two lyrics are concerned, it is generally agreed that the *Ṛtusaṁhāra* must have been composed earlier than the *Meghadūta*, for the former seems to be a composition of his youthful days, while the latter which is a work of his maturity clearly shows his poetic art at its best in the handling of metre, imagery and expression. As regards his dramas, there cannot be any manner of doubt that the *Śākuntala*, which has won universal eclat, is Kālidāsa's best and last play. However, there is some controversy with regard to the chronological sequence of the other two plays. A majority of modern scholars who regard the *Mālavikāgnimitra* as the first play of Kālidāsa advance the arguments that in the prologue of this play Kālidāsa deems it necessary to justify why the drama of a modern playwright (Kālidāsa) is going to be presented at the spring-festival by ignoring the compositions of such renowned dramatists as Bhāsa, Saumilla and Kaviputra; and that no such justification is offered in the prologue of the *Vikramorvaśīya*. Another argument advanced in support of this view is that Kālidāsa's dramatic art appears to be more developed in the *Vikramorvaśīya* than in the *Mālavikāgnimitra*. The other scholars who hold the opposite view argue that in the prologue of the *Vikramorvaśīya* Kālidāsa simply mentions the performance of a new drama before a learned assembly which has already witnessed and enjoyed the compositions of earlier dramatists, but does not feel it necessary to justify the same, whereas he takes great pains in the prologue of the *Mālavikāgnimitra* to defend the presentation of a play composed by a modern dramatist and even goes to the extent of dubbing his critics fools who are led by the opinions of others without assessing independently the merits and demerits of old and new compositions,[9] because his first drama *Vikramorvaśīya* must have been unduly criticised by his contemporaries. However, a comparison of the *Mālavikāgnimitra* and the *Vikramorvaśīya* in respect of their dramatic qualities makes it abundantly clear that the latter shows a definite development in Kālidāsa's dramatic art and poetic achievement. In fact the *Vikramorvaśīya* is a precursor of his masterpiece *Śākuntala* (*infra*, Chapter IV). By the time he composed the *Śākuntala* Kālidāsa had not only perfected his dramatic art but had also won the appreciation and applause of his contemporaries. Therefore, in the prologue of his last play he displays his humility by saying that he does not consider his knowledge of dramatic representation adequate until and unless it satisfies the scholars.[10]

Similarly there is a difference of opinion in regard to the chronological sequence of the epics *Raghuvaṁśa* and the *Kumārasambhava*. The predominant view is that the *Kumārasambhava* was composed by the poet in his youth, while the *Raghuvaṁśa* which refers to the Yoga philosophy and employs grammatical similes is the product of his mature age. On the contrary, some scholars, who regard the *Kumārasambhava* as the final composition of Kālidāsa, advance the arguments that this epic is far superior to the *Raghuvaṁśa* in poetic excellence, and that the death of the poet might have resulted in the abrupt ending of the *Kumārasambhava* at its eighth Canto, because the following nine Cantos which have not been commented upon by the famous commentators Mallinātha and Aruṇagirinātha are obviously spurious and later accretions as attested by the inferiority of their style, expressions and ideas. Another argument advanced in support of the priority of the *Raghuvaṁśa* is that in its opening verse the poet, being a novice in poetry, prays for the success of his poetic art, while he does not deem it necessary to do so in the *Kumārasambhava* because his reputation as a poet had been fully established prior to its composition. This argument can be countered by the plea that, since the composition of the *Kumārasambhava* which was begun without offering a prayer in the beginning had to be left incomplete after the eighth Canto due to adverse criticism, the poet deemed it necessary to offer a prayer in the beginning of the *Raghuvaṁśa* for its successful completion. Moreover, a prayer in the beginning of a literary work does not betray the poet's lack of confidence, but it shows his maturity; for Kālidāsa prays to Śiva not only in the beginning of the *Śākuntala* but also in its concluding stanza for his final emancipation. There is no doubt that the *Kumārasambhava* excels the *Raghuvaṁśa* in the description of youthful beauty, whereas the latter is superior to the former in demonstrating his vast learning and mature outlook. Thus his youthful imagination is reflected in the *Kumārasambhava* and the maturity of his thought and style in the *Raghuvaṁśa*. A careful comparison of slightly different verses connected with the common verses[11] of the *Kumārasambhava* and the *Raghuvaṁśa* reveals Kālidāsa's more polished and mature style in the latter. For instance, in the *Raghuvaṁśa*[12] Kālidāsa has substantially improved upon his similar verse of the *Kumārasambhava*[13] justifying the choice of a worthy match. In the *Kumārasambhava* Kālidāsa expresses the youthful idea that even that woman who may become a slave of Śiva is blessed and what to say of that one who may attain his lap, while the poet drops this idea in the corresponding verse of the *Raghuvaṁśa* in spite of some common words, and introduces instead a simile to compare Indumatī with Lakṣmī and Aja with Nārāyaṇa. Although the poet has included in the *Raghuvaṁśa* so many other verses from the *Kumārasambhava* in this context without any change, the maturity of his age and thought did not allow him to repeat here the above-mentioned youthful idea expressed in the *Kumārasambhava*. As a result of the further development of his style Kālidāsa in the *Raghuvaṁśa*[14] (VII, 12) substitutes "*tā rāghavaṁ dṛṣṭibhir āpibantyaḥ*" for his earlier expression[15] "*tam ekadṛśyaṁ nayanaiḥ pibantyaḥ*" (*Kumārasambhava* VII, 64). The rest of the verse remains unchanged. Instances can be multiplied to prove Kālidāsa's maturity of thought and style in the *Raghuvaṁśa* in comparison with the *Kumārasambhava*.

Kālidāsa has exercised tremendous influence on the later Sanskrit literature—rather on the entire later Indian literature. We have fully discussed below in Chapter II the expressions and phrases borrowed verbatim by Aśvaghoṣa from the works of Kālidāsa. The earliest paleographical evidence of Kālidāsa's influence is found in a Sanskrit inscription written by Vatsabhaṭṭi (473 A.D.) in the Sun-temple at Mandasor. In this inscription Vatsabhaṭṭi imitates the ideas and expressions contained in Kālidāsa's lyrics—the *Ṛtusaṁhāra* and the *Meghadūta*. Kālidāsa's influence is discernible in several Sanskrit plays, such as the *Priyadarśikā*, the *Ratnāvalī*, the *Karpūramañjarī* and the *Viddhaśālabhañjikā* in which Kālidāsa's theme of a married king's secret love with a damsel living under the protection of his queen, as dramatized in the *Mālavikāgnimitra*, has been adopted with suitable modifications. Even Bhavabhūti, who is noted for his originality of treatment of nature and human sentiments, betrays in his dramas the influence of Kālidāsa's works. A large number of *dūtakāvyas*, such as the *Pavana-dūta*, the *Bhramara-dūta*, the *Chātaka-dūta*, the *Śuka-dūta*, the *Chakravāka-dūta*, the *Kokila-dūta* have been composed by the later writers in imitation of Kālidāsa's *Meghadūta*. Kālidāsā's theme of sending an exiled lover's message through a cloud has been adopted by the famous German poet-playwright Schiller in his *Maria Sturat* (Act III, Sc. 1) in which the captive Queen of Scots requests the clouds to greet on her behalf the land of her youth in the course of their southward flight. After reading Kālidāsa's masterpiece *Śākuntala* in German translation, Goethe composed the prologue of his famous play *Faust* on the model of this Sanskrit play where the stage-manager and his wife (the chief actress) converse about the play to be staged, its author, and the opening scene.

Kālidāsa who represented a rare combination of the best qualities of head and heart was a peerless creative genius endowed with a lofty vision, broad outlook, deep learning, fine culture and consummate literary skill. A cursory perusal of Kālidāsa's works reveals his mastery over various important branches of learning such as the Vedas, Upaniṣads, Vedāṅgas, Epics, Purāṇas, Dharmaśāstra, Arthaśāstra, philosophy, grammar, prosody, poetics, dramaturgy, erotics, astronomy, music, dance, painting and medicine. But he bears his learning lightly like a fragrant flower and refrains from pedantry. His learning lends dignity and grace to his poetry and does not mar its charm by ostentation.

Kālidāsa's lofty vision transcends all barriers of time and space and perceives the essential unity of diverse constituents of the vast universe. Therefore, his works portray a constant communion between the denizens of heaven and earth. Celestial nymphs are depicted as descending on the earth and falling in love with mortals, and several terrestrial kings are shown as travelling between heaven and earth at the invitation of Lord Indra. The gods are described in his works as concerned with the affairs of this world, interfering with them, and expressing their joy and sorrow at certain important events taking place in the world. In this respect Kālidāsa is undoubtedly indebted to the Vedic and Epic literature. Kālidāsa's works glorify the Vedic and Epic ideas and ideals pertaining to the performance of sacrifices and sacraments, and the achievement of the four principal aims of life through its four stages called *Āśramas*. In the beginning of his all the three plays Kālidāsa offers obeisance to Lord Śiva, and prays to both Śiva and Pārvatī in the opening verse of the *Raghuvaṁśa*. Moreover, the god Śiva is highly eulogized by the poet in his *Kumārasambhava*. Thus Kālidāsa appears to be a devotee of *Aṣṭamūrti*[16] Śiva. However, unlike the later sectarian Purāṇas and other texts, Kālidāsa does not seek to establish Śiva's superiority to the other two gods of Hindu trinity, as our poet highly praises both Brahman and Viṣṇu and offers prayers to the former in the *Kumārasambhava*[17] and to the latter in the *Raghuvaṁśa*[18]. Besides, Kālidāsa regards the three gods—Brahman, Viṣṇu and Śiva—as three different aspects of the same eternal Reality without any distinction of priority or posteriority, inferiority or superiority.[19] Like the Ṛgvedic seer Dīrghatamas,[20] Kālidāsa sees fundamental unity in diverse names and forms of the Supreme Being. It is a unique achievement of Kālidāsa's genius that his works contain not only charming delineation of Nature, beauty and human sentiments but also embody the philosophy of spiritual elevation and beatitude.

Notes and References

1. लिप्ता मधुद्रवेणासन्यस्य निर्विषया गिरः ।
   तेनेदं वर्त्म वैदर्भं कालिदासेन शोधितम् ॥
   (*Avanti-Sundarī-Kathā*, Introductory Verse 15).

2. निर्गतासु न वा कस्य कालिदासस्य सूक्तिषु ।
   प्रीतिर्मधुरसान्द्रासु मञ्जरीष्विव जायते ॥
   (*Harṣacharita*, Introductory Verse 16).

3. Max Müller in his well-known work "*A History of Ancient Sanrkrit Literature*" (Varanasi, 1968) p.1, quotes Goethe's famous epigram and translates it as follows :

"Willt Du die Blüthe des frühen,
die Früchte des späteren Jahres,
Willt Du, was reizt und entzückt,
Willt Du was sättigt und nährt,
Willt Du den Himmel, die Erde
mit einem Namen begreifen,
Nenn ich, Sacontala, Dich, Und so ist Alles gesagt."

"Wilt thou the blossoms of spring
and the fruits that are later in season,
Wilt thou have charms and delights,
wilt thou have strength and support,
Wilt thou with one short word
encompass the earth and the heaven,
All is said if I name only, Sacontala, thee."

4. Translated into English by Nagendra Nath Gupta in *The Modern Review*, 1932, pp. 622-23.
5. See his work "*The Birth-place of Kālidāsa*", Delhi University Publication No. I, 1926.
6. In KS. VII, 39 *Kālī*, *Kapālābharaṇā* "wearing an ornament of skulls", is mentioned only as one of the members of Śiva's bridal procession.
7. Mbh. XIII, 24, 25.
8. Although Mallinātha in his commentary on the *Meghadūta* (Pūrvamegha, 50) explains *Kanakhala* as a mountain, the Mbh. describes it as a *Tīrtha* (III, 84, 30; XVI, 25, 13) as well as a mountain (III, 135, 5).
9. पुराणमित्येव न साधु सर्वं
   न चापि काव्यं नवमित्यवद्यम् ।
   सन्तः परीक्ष्यान्यतरद्भजन्ते
   मूढः परप्रत्ययनेयबुद्धिः ॥
   (Māl. I, 2).
10. आ परितोषाद्विदुषां न साधु मन्ये प्रयोगविज्ञानम् ।
    बलवदपि शिक्षितानामात्मन्यप्रत्ययं चेतः ॥
    (Śāk. I, 2).
11. KS. VII, 56-66.73=Ragh. VII, 5-14.19.
12. स्थाने वृता भूपतिभिः परोक्षैः स्वयंवरं साधुममंस्त भोज्या ।
    पद्मेव नारायणमन्यथासौ लभेत कान्तं कथमात्मतुल्यम् ॥
    (Ragh. VII, 13).
13. स्थाने तपो दुश्चरमेतदर्थमपर्णया पेलवयापि तप्तम् ।
    या दास्यमप्यस्य लभेत नारी सा स्यात्कृतार्था किमुतांकशय्याम् ॥
    (KS. VII, 65).
14. ता राघवं दृष्टिभिरापिबन्त्यो नार्यो न जग्मुर्विषयान्तराणि ।
    तथा हि शेषेन्द्रियवृत्तिरासां सर्वात्मना चक्षुरिव प्रविष्टा ॥
    (Ragh. VII, 12).
15. तमेकदृश्यं नयनैः पिबन्त्यो नार्यो न जग्मुर्विषयान्तराणि ।
    तथा हि शेषेन्द्रियवृत्तिरासां सर्वात्मना चक्षुरिव प्रविष्टा ॥
    (KS. VII, 64).
16. *Aṣṭamūrti* "eight-formed" Śiva is glorified in the Śāk. (I, 1) KS. (VI, 26; VII, 76.87) and the Ragh. (II, 35). According to Kālidāsa (Śāk. I, 1), the five elements, the sun, the moon and the sacrificing priest are the eight forms of Śiva. Śiva's epithet *Aṣṭamūrti* is mentioned in the Mbh. (III, 49, 8) also.
17. KS. II, 2 15.
18. Ragh. X, 15-33.

19. नमस्त्रिमूर्तये तुभ्यं प्राक्सृष्टेः केवलात्मने ।
गुणत्रयविभागाय पश्चाद्भेदमुपेयुषे ॥
(KS. II, 4).

एकैव मूर्तिर्बिभिदे त्रिधा सा सामान्यमेषां प्रथमावरत्वम् ।
विष्णोर्हरस्तस्य हरिः कदाचिद्वेधास्तयोस्तावपि धातुराद्यौ ॥
(KS. VII, 44).

20. इन्द्रं मित्रं वरुणमग्निमाहु—
रथो दिव्यः स सुपर्णो गरुत्मान् ।
एकं सद्विप्रा बहुधा वद—
न्त्यग्निं यमं मातरिश्वानमाहुः ॥
(RV. I, 164, 46).

2

The Date of Kalidasa

There is a sharp difference of opinion among scholars with regard to the date of Kālidāsa, and it is beyond the scope of the present work to examine here critically in detail all the theories and controversies on the subject. We shall, therefore, content ourselves with briefly discussing here only important views on Kālidāsa's date which oscilates between second century B.C. and sixth century A.D. The lowest limit of his date is fixed by his praise in Bāṇa's *Harṣacharita* and in Ravikīrti's Aihole inscription. Since Bāṇa flourished in the reign of King Harṣa (606-647 A.D.) and the Aihole inscripti n is dated 634 A.D., it obviously leads us to the inference that a period of at least a few centuries must have elapsed by the beginning of the seventh century A.D. when Kālidāsa's fame had spread far and wide. The lower limit of Kālidāsa's date is further pushed up by the Mandasor inscription (473 A.D.) which clearly shows that its author Vatsabhaṭṭi who imitates the *Meghadūta* (Pūrva, 66) and the *Ṛtusaṁhāra* (V, 2-3) is indebted to the immortal poet. The evidence adduced from Vatsabhaṭṭi's inscription, the Aihole inscription and Bāṇa's *Harṣacharita* precludes all such theories (including Max Müller's Renaissance Theory) as assign Kālidāsa to the sixth century A.D. or to a later date. As regards the theory declaring Kālidāsa to be a contemporary of the Śuṅga King Agnimitra (2nd century B.C.) whose secret love with Mālavikā is dramatized in the famous play *Mālavikāgnimitra* (*infra*, Chapter IV), it may be pointed out that no court-poet dare make satirical and adverse remarks against his patron King. But in this drama Kālidāsa puts some uncharitable remarks against Agnimitra in the mouth of his queens Irāvatī and

Dhāriṇī. Therefore, the theory which assigns Kālidāsa to the second century B.C. on the basis of Agnimitra's mild praise in the last verse of the *Mālavikāgnimitra* lacks plausibility.

The predominant view about Kālidāsa's date is that he flourished during the reign of King Chandragupta II (c. 380-413 A.D.) who assumed the title of *Vikramāditya* after onquering northern and western parts of India and who shifted his capital to Ujjayinī. It is claimed that this view conforms to the tradition which makes Kālidāsa as a court-poet of King Vikramāditya of Ujjayinī. It is further argued by the advocates of this theory that prosperity, power and glory depicted in Kālidāsa's works reflect the triumphant conditions of the Gupta period. Some scholars read the conquests of Samudragupta into Raghu's *Digvijaya* described in the *Raghuvaṁśa*,[1] the title Vikramāditya of Chandragupta II into the play *Vikramorvaśīya*,[2] the birth of Chandragupta's son Kumāragupta into the epic *Kumārasambhava*,[3] and a covert reference to Samudragupta's horse-sacrifice into the mention of the horse-sacrifice in the *Mālavikāgnimitra*.[4] It is also urged by the supporters of this theory that several motifs of the Gupta art, such as the decoration of door-jambs with the figures of conch and lotus or with the figures of the Gaṅgā and the Yamunā, the figure of Kārttikeya riding a peacock, and the representation of Viṣṇu's weapons in dwarfish human forms, find graphic description in the works of Kālidāsa.[5]

The tradition, that associates Kālidāsa with King Vikramāditya *Śakāri* (vanquisher of the Śakas) of Ujjayinī and enumerates him among the nine jewels of Vikramāditya's court, is late and worthless, as pointed out by Keith[6]; and its source, the *Jyotirvidābharaṇa*, is a very late work.[7] This tradition is so flexible that some scholars, who regard the legendary King Vikramāditya as the founder of the Vikrama era (57 B.C.), use this argument to assign Kālidāsa to the first century B.C., while others utilize the same tradition to place Kālidāsa in the fourth century A.D. by identifying the legendary King Vikramāditya with Chandragupta II who had assumed the title of Vikramāditya after vanquishing the Śaka satraps of Malwa, Gujarat and Kathiawar; and this very tradition is also used by a few scholars to place Kālidāsa in the sixth century A.D. by identifying the legendary King Vikramāditya with King Yaśodharman of Malwa who defeated the Hūṇas. The said tradition betrays its anachronism by naming Dhanvantari, Kṣapaṇaka, Amarasiṁha, Śaṅku, Vetāla Bhaṭṭa, Ghaṭakarpara, Kālidāsa, Varāhamihira and Vararuchi as nine jewels of the court of the legendary King Vikramāditya. So this tradition about Kālidāsa is as unreliable as the one contained in Ballālasena's *Bhojaprabandha* (16th century A.D.) which mentions Kālidāsa as one of the nine jewels of the court of King Bhoja of Dhārā of the eleventh century A.D. along with several later poets such as Daṇḍin, Bāṇa, Bhavabhūti and Śrīharṣa. It is well known to every student of the history of Sanskrit literature that all these literary figures cannot be contemporaries. It is thus obvious that no reliance can be placed on such unhistorical traditions in fixing the date of Kālidāsa.

It cannot be gainsaid that a period of peace, prosperity, victory, and glory is reflected in Kālidāsa's works—especially in the *Raghuvaṁśa*. However, it is a moot point whether the poet is depicting an ideal picture of society on the model of the *Rāmāyaṇa* or he is portraying a picture of his own times. Can it be historically proved that the city of Ujjayinī, with which Kālidāsa seems to be associated according to internal evidence, never witnessed peace, prosperity and glory between the first century B.C. and the fourth century A.D. except under the rule of Chandragupta II? If we free ourselves from the preconception that Kālidāsa flourished during the Gupta period and analyse the texts objectively and dispassionately, there is nothing positive in Kālidāsa's works to suggest that Samudragupta's great conquests are reflected in Raghu's *Digvijaya*, or the birth of the Gupta prince Kumāragupta is hinted at in the title of the epic *Kumārasambhava*, or the royal title *Vikramāditya* of Chandragupta II is alluded to in the play *Vikramorvaśīya*, or Samudragupta's horse-sacrifice is covertly referred to in the *Mālavikāgnimitra* which mentions the horse-sacrifice performed by Puṣyamitra. Although Kālidāsa's description of Raghu's *Digvijaya* is original, yet it cannot be denied that he must have drawn inspiration in this respect from the two Epics, the *Rāmāyaṇa* and the *Mahābhārata*, to which he is undoubtedly indebted in various ways. It is noteworthy that the names of most of the countries, rivers, hills, tribes, etc., mentioned in the description of Raghu's *Digvijaya* are met with in the description of Pāṇḍavas' *Digvijaya*,[8] Arjuna's expedition in the course of the wanderings of the horse let loose for the horse-sacrifice,[9] and in Vālmīki's description of monkeys' search for Sītā in all directions.[10] It is quite likely that Kālidāsa had before him these epic descriptions of various parts of India at the time of composing his own description of Raghu's *Digvijaya*. So it is unjustifiable to read the conquests of the Gupta kings into this description.

Since the performance of the horse-sacrifice by Puṣyamitra is a historical fact, I see no justification for reading a covert reference to Samudragupta's horse-sacrifice into the mention of the Aśvamedha in the *Mālavikāgnimitra*. Similarly there seems to be no valid reason for reading the title Vikramāditya of Chandragupta II into the *Vikramorvaśīya*; nor is there any indication that the title of the epic *Kumārasambhava* hints in any way a compliment on the birth of the Gupta prince Kumāragupta. If the poet had really intended any such compliment, he would have definitely made it explicit in his work. The similarity of art motifs met with in Kālidāsa's works and Gupta art does not necessarily imply that Kālidāsa borrowed them from Gupta art. It is quite likely that such art motifs were already in vogue in Kālidāsa's times and were later adopted in the Gupta art also. Similarly there is no weight in the argument that the frequent use of the √*gup* "to protect" in Kālidāsa's works indicates his association with the Gupta kings, for he employs in this sense several other roots such as √*trai*, √*rakṣ* and √*pā*, besides √*gup*. Moreover, the use of any root or noun cannot prove the association of any author with any king.

Kālidāsa's reference to the defeat of the Hūṇas by Raghu[11] in the vicinity of the river *Sindhu*[12] (according to one reading) is used as an argument by some scholars against assigning an early date, say 1st or 2nd century B.C., to the poet on the ground that the Hūṇas were nowhere near the river Indus at such an early date. However, this argument is rendered partly effete by the fact that some MSS of the *Raghuvaṁśa* contain, in place of *Sindhu*, the variant reading *Vaṅkṣū* which is identified by most of the modern scholars with the river Oxus of Bactria. The argument advanced in support of the reading *Sindhu* is that the famous commentator Mallinātha accepts this reading, explains *Sindhu* as a river of Kashmir, and cites from the *Amarakośa* the word *kāśmīra-janman* meaning "saffron" which is cultivated in Kashmir. Besides, the commentator Dinakara Miśra observes that the idea of saffron sticking to the manes of Raghu's horses is justified on the ground that saffron is mostly cultivated in Kashmir. But the supporters of the reading *Vaṅkṣū* advance the plea that saffron was also cultivated in Bactria irrigated by the river Oxus, because the word *Bāhlīka*, ancient Indian name of Bactria, is enumerated in the *Amarakośa* (II, 123-124) among the synonyms of *kuṅkuma* "saffron." Moreover, Kṣīrasvāmin (circa 11th century A.D.), a commentator of the *Amarakośa*, observes that the word *Bāhlīka* denotes saffron on account of its cultivation in the *Bāhlīka* country as attested in the *Raghuvaṁśa* that the horses of Raghu's cavalry shook off saffron sticking to their manes. The balance of probability favours the reading *Vaṅkṣū* instead of *Sindhu*. Besides, it is very difficult to say with absolute certainty that Kālidāsa in his *Raghuvaṁśa* is accurately referring to the settlements of the Hūṇas in his times, and that his stray reference to them is not based either on second-hand information derived from travellers coming from the west or from the pool of popular information current in India at that time. The Epics also mention the Hūṇas, and it cannot be established with certainty that all those portions of the Epics which speak of the Hūṇas are later interpolations. Anyhow, no firm opinion about the date of Kālidāsa can be expressed on the basis of such doubtful references in his works.

A few attempts have been made to fix Kālidāsa's date on the basis of some supposed astronomical references in his works. For instance, it is argued by some scholars that Kālidāsa's mention of *Jāmitra* (KS. VII,1), which in their opinion has been derived from the Greek astronomical term *diametron*, indicates a date later than the introduction of this Greek term in India. But this argument is beset with two difficulties. First, according to one view, the term *āmitraj* has been derived from the Sanskrit word *jāmi* and not from the said Greek term. Secondly, even if it is conceded that the term *jāmitra* has been borrowed from Greek astronomy, there is no unanimity among scholars with regard to the time of introduction of this Greek term in India. Some scholars assign Kālidāsa to the sixth century A.D. by placing an arbitrary astronomical interpretation on the second verse of the *Meghadūta*, especially on the variant reading *praśama-divase* for *prathama-divase*, and also on the second half of verse 22 of Act VII of the *Śākuntala*: "as the constellation *Rohiṇī* comes into conjunction with the moon after a lunar eclipse." No exact astronomical calculation concerning Kālidāsa's date is possible from such general statements. Nor is there any indication to prove that the above-mentioned statement of the *Śākuntala* refers to an actual total lunar eclipse as assumed by the advocates of this hypothesis.

Only unimpeachable internal evidence corroborated by inscriptional, archaeological and literary data can be really helpful in fixing approximately the poet's date. We have already discussed above briefly Bāṇa's laudatory reference to Kālidāsa in the *Harṣacharita* and also the inscriptional evidence bearing on his date.

Now we shall discuss in detail the literary evidence available from Aśvaghoṣa's *Buddhacharita* and *Saundarananda* to determine the relative chronology of Kālidāsa and Aśvaghoṣa. In addition to close similarities of ideas, situations and descriptions, the verbatim agreements between the works of these two authors are far too many to be lightly brushed aside as merely fortuitous or inconsequential. It is abundantly clear from a careful comparison of their works that either of the two poets studied the works of the other and borrowed ideas and expressions from his works. Let us present here all the relevant facts and draw the logical conclusions from them without any preconception.

However, in this connection we have to reckon, first of all, with the views of a large number of modern scholars who have been persistently labouring for nearly a century under the preconceived notion that, since Aśvaghoṣa is earlier than Kālidāsa, the latter must have been indebted to the former for similar ideas and expressions. E.B. Cowell who published the *Buddhacharita* from Oxford in 1893 was the first Western scholar to propound this thesis. So the learned scholar remarks[13]: "I can hardly doubt that Kālidāsa's finished picture was suggested by the rough but vigorous outlines in Aśvaghoṣa; he was the Buddhist Ennius who gave the first inspiration to the Hindu Virgil." Following Cowell, some Western scholars have gone to the extent of suggesting that the imitation of Aśvaghoṣa's *Buddhacharita* is found in the *Rāmāyaṇa* also. Comparing the description of Rāvaṇa's harem at night in the *Rāmāyaṇa* with a similar description of the night scene in the *Buddhacharita* (V, 47-62) at the time of Siddhārtha's secret departure to the forest from his palace, M. Winternitz observes:[14] "The nightly seraglio-scene (V, 9-11) is described vividly in the style of ornate poetry, and forcibly recalls the description in the Buddha legend, where Prince Siddhārtha, surrounded by his wives, awakens at the hour of midnight, and is seized with disgust at sensual pleasure. The similarity of the situation and of the description is sufficiently striking to justify the supposition that it is an imitation of the description in Aśvaghoṣa's *Buddhacharita* (V, 47ff.). For as E.B. Cowell rightly remarks (in the preface to his edition of the *Buddhacharita*), this scene forms an essential part of the Buddha legend, while in the *Rāmāyaṇa* it is only an entirely unnecessary embellishment. Of course we must not ascribe the piece to Vālmīki himself, but the imitation must be ascribed to a later interpolation." This view has been refuted by several scholars including A.B. Keith who asserts:[15] "Nor does it seem reasonable to deny that the description of the aspect of women of the harem in sleep is based on the portraiture of Rāvaṇa's harem." There is nothing to indicate that this portion of the *Rāmāyaṇa* is a later interpolation.

There is abundant evidence in Aśvaghoṣa's above-mentioned two works to prove conclusively that he was not only influenced by the *Rāmāyaṇa* in his ideas, style, similes and expressions but he also borrowed some phrases verbatim from the Epic. He mentions Vālmīki as *ādikavi*[16] and *dhīmān*[17], and compares Chhandaka's return to Kapilavastu without Siddhārtha to Sumantra's return to Ayodhyā without Rāma,[18] and Śuddhodana's plight to that of Daśaratha[19]. The instances of close parallelisms between the *Rāmāyaṇa* and the *Buddhacharita* clearly prove that Aśvaghoṣa has borrowed these passages verbatim from the Epic and made slight alterations in them.[20] There is also a striking similarity between some phrases contained in the *Rāmāyaṇa* and the *Saundarananda*.[21] The foregoing facts leave no manner of doubt that Aśvaghoṣa, who is highly indebted to Vālmīki for ideas, similes and descriptions, has borrowed verbatim a number of phrases from the *Rāmāyaṇa* and has slightly modified them here and there.

Besides the *Rāmāyaṇa*, several other important works such as the *Śvetāśvatara Upaniṣad*, the *Kaṭha Upaniṣad*, and the *Mahābhārata* (especially the *Bhagavadgītā*) have also been drawn upon by Aśvaghoṣa who has lifted some stanzas or parts of some stanzas from them with slight alterations. In addition to certain similarities in ideas between the *Śvetāśvatara Upaniṣad* and Aśvaghoṣa's works, one passage from the former has been borrowed almost verbatim in the *Saundarananda*[22] with slight alterations to suit the context. In this connection E.H. Johnston rightly observes that the resemblance of *Saundarananda* (XVI, 17) to the *Śvetāśvatara Upaniṣad* can hardly be fortuitous.[23] Similarly the first half of a stanza[24] from the *Kaṭha Upaniṣad* has been suitably altered and a simile[25] from it has been borrowed almost verbatim by Aśvaghoṣa in his *Buddhacharita*. The parallelisms of ideas and expressions between the *Mahābhārata* and Aśvaghoṣa's works are far too many to be fully dealt with here. Numerous legends and characters of the Great Epic have been frequently utilized by Aśvaghoṣa. There can be no doubt that Aśvaghoṣa is highly indebted to the *Mahābhārata*. Only a few instances demonstrating almost verbatim agreemrnt between the *Mahābhārata* and Aśvaghoṣa's works are cited in the Notes[26] appended to this Chapter. Aśvaghoṣa has borrowed verbatim a number of passages from the *Bhagavadgītā* also with minor alterations here and there.[27] Besides, we find a very close similarity between a verse of the *Buddhacharita* and the one contained in the play *Pratijñā-Yaugandharāyaṇa* ascribed to Bhāsa.[28]

It follows from the foregoing discussion that Aśvaghoṣa betrays the tendency of borrowing from the earlier works not only ideas, similes, and themes of poetic descriptions but also verbatim phrases and passages with such slight alterations as can hardly conceal his blatant borrowing. On the contrary, there is no evidence to show that Kālidāsa has borrowed verbatim any phrase or passage from any of the earlier works such as the Upaniṣads and the Epics, though he had fully mastered the then existing Sanskrit works and imbibed their thought and spirit. But so far as his expression is concerned, it is remarkably original, polished and felicitous. In the case of numerous verbatim agreements between Kālidāsa and Aśvaghoṣa, the crucial point at issue is whether the latter whose works betray a strong tendency of verbatim borrowing from several earlier works is the borrower or the borrowing has been made by the former who in that unlikely case chose to borrow verbatim phrases from only Aśvaghoṣa's works and not from any other work of the vast Sanskrit literature. The balance of probability suggests that Aśvaghoṣa, who is in the habit of lifting phrases and passages verbatim from the earlier works, must have exploited Kālidāsa's works for elegant expressions and charming descriptions. It is admitted on all hands that Kālidāsa's approach to poetry is purely artistic and literary, whereas Aśvaghoṣa, being an avowed Buddhist preacher, subordinates poetry to his religious preachings and candidly declares in the concluding stanzas of his *Saundarananda* that this work embodying the import of salvation has been composed by him in poetic form, not for aesthetic pleasure, but to attract towards complete quietude the minds of hearers attached to other things; that the adoption of poetic form in this work is intended to attract people towards salvation, just as a bitter medicine is made palatabe through the mixture of honey; that the truth leading to salvation has been here presented by him in the garb of poetry in view of the fact that people mostly indulge in the enjoyment of sensual pleasures and remain averse to salvation; and that only the truth leading to tranquillity should be carefully grasped from this work, leaving out its attractive amorous content.[29] It is evident from Aśvaghoṣa's statement that he employs the poetic form of composition in his works to subserve the ends of his religious preaching. In order to achieve this object he does not hesitate to borrow verbatim phrases, stanzas, or themes of descriptions from the earlier works available to him. It seems highly unlikely that Kālidāsa, who has written poetry for the sake of poetry, would have borrowed verbatim passages and phrases from only a religious preacher who himself was a confirmed borrower, and would have refrained from following in his (Aśvaghoṣa's) footsteps in making such verbatim borrowing from the other well-known works of the earlier Sanskrit literature. If Kālidāsa had resorted to such a large-scale verbatim borrowing of phrases and passages from Aśvoghoṣa, the former would not have been able to escape entirely the latter's influence in respect of his Buddhistic ideas and ideology. But no Buddhistic influence is discernible in Kālidāsa's works. We find no substance in the attempts to see Aśvaghoṣa's influence on Kālidāsa's language.[30] On the contrary, Aśvaghoṣa's works betray the influence of Kālidāsa's language, and the awareness of this fact can render great help in correcting some corrupt readings of Aśvaghoṣa's works and in interpreting some obscure passages contained in them.[31] Besides, Aśvaghoṣa's allusion to the story of Kāma's attempt to induce Śiva for Pārvatī seems to be more in accordance with Kālidāsa's *Kumārasambhava* than with the Epics, since none of the extant Purāṇic versions of the story can be regarded as older than the *Kumārasambhava.* In the B. (XIII, 16) Kāma says to himself after shooting his arrow at the Buddha: "Even the god Śambhu pierced with the arrow became agitated with love towards Himālaya's daughter, but this man (Buddha) does not care for that arrow. Is he heartless or is it not the same arrow?" According to Aśvaghoṣa's cryptic allusion, Śiva was pierced by Kāma with the arrow, whereas in the version contained in the *Kumārasambhava* (III, 66-72) Kāma is burnt to ashes as soon as he aims his arrow at Śiva whose mind becomes agitated after casting a glance at Pārvatī's beautiful face, and later (KS.V) she wins Śiva's heart through her austerities. In his cryptic allusion Aśvaghoṣa seems to have introduced this change in the story in order to prove the Buddha's superiority to Śiva in withstanding Kāma. Moreover, Aśvaghoṣa's reference to the performance of necessary rites by Vālmīki for Sītā's two sons appears to be an imitation of Kālidāsa's *Raghuvaṁśa* in regard to the idea as well as its wording,[32] because the Uttarakāṇḍa of the *Rāmāyaṇa* does not afford such a close parallelism in this respect. These references betray Aśvaghoṣa's close acquaintance with Kālidāsa's two epics.

A major argument advanced by the advocates of Aśvaghoṣa's priority to Kālidāsa is that the latter's developed, refined and polished style in comparison with the primitive, 'pedestrian' and repetitive style of the former betokens Kālidāsa's posteriority to Aśvaghoṣa.[33] Comparing Kālidāsa's style with that of Aśvaghoṣa, Keith observes[34]: "Kālidāsa exhibits the influence of increased refinement of style in his dramas, just as in his epics he normally avoids the pedestrian traits which are easily to be found in the epics of his forerunner Aśvaghoṣa." Referring to the baffling contrasts in Aśvaghoṣa's style, Johnston remarks[35]: "Aśvaghoṣa is a writer of baffling contrasts, on the one hand the literary artist as story-teller, preacher and poet, on the other the scholar anxious to conform with all the rules and to parade his knowledge. The possession of good qualities implies a liability to the corresponding defects, and among a people who treasured intelligence and learning it is not surprising to find some who lapsed at times, like the Buddhist poet, into pedantry. For if his matter is excellent, his manner is often disconcerting." The same scholar further on characterises Aśvaghoṣa as a 'primitive' in his art, and regards his intricacy and elaboration as those of the primitive and not of a sophisticated writer like Kālidāsa.[36] Similarly Gurner also describes Aśvaghoṣa's style as a mixture of naive efforts and artificial embellishment.[37] Most of the modern scholars admit that Aśvaghoṣa cannot match Kālidāsa in poetic skill and elegance. But a poet's superiority to another in poetic art and style does not necessarily imply that he must be later than his inferior counterpart, and that his superiority in this respect must be the result of his having improved upon the disconcerting, disharmonious, and repetitive style of an inferior predecessor. In poetic art it is only the innate genius and culture of a poet which displays its original excellence in his poetry. Mere imitation of another poet does not lead to any improvement in poetry, and easily betrays its true character. If the posteriority of a poet marks his superiority to his predecessors in poetic art, all those poets who followed Kālidāsa should have excelled him. But it is not so. It cannot be gainsaid that in certain respects Vālmīki remains unsurpassed even by Kālidāsa, not to speak of Aśvaghoṣa whose poetic art is certainly much inferior to that of the *Ādikavi*. Therefore, the inferiority or superiority of a writer's art and style cannot be accepted as a reliable criterion for fixing his relative chronology. The principle of evolution cannot be applied to art in the same way as it is applied to physical sciences.

A minute and critical examination of the parallelisms between Kālidāsa and Aśvaghoṣa, as attempted below, will reveal the real reasons underlying "the baffling contrasts" of Aśvaghoṣa's art as well as "the mixture of naive efforts and artificial embellishment" in his style. Since Aśvaghoṣa, unlike Kālidāsa, has not written poetry out of any aesthetic urge but has only given the poetic garb to his religious preachings, he (Aśvaghoṣa) has not hesitated to lift verbatim passages, phrases and descriptions from well-known earlier works and has thus made his poetry a medley of heterogeneous styles and matter ranging from the Upaniṣads to Kālidāsa's works. Moreover, in his anxiety to conceal his verbatim borrowings Aśvaghoṣa has made such changes in the borrowed passages as have marred his art and made the style of the altered passages look inferior to that of the original, as shown below.

1. Describing the birth of Raghu, Kālidāsa says that as soon as the natural radiance issuing from the boy of auspicious birth spread around his mother's lying-in couch, the night lamps suddenly became bereft of light as if they were painted in a picture.[38] Kālidāsa's wording in the above description of the night lamps has been borrowed verbatim by Aśvaghoṣa with slight alteration and applied to the description of some women of Kapilavastu on the return of Chhandaka and the horse without Siddhārtha as follows[39]: "Other women bereft of light stood stunned (without the acts of moving, breathing and weeping) as if they were painted in a picture." The use of the epithet *hata-tviṣaḥ* "bereft of light" (applied to the night lamps by Kālidāsa) for women in the *Buddhacharita* demonstrates Aśvaghoṣa's naive effort to fit this epithet somehow into his work, though

the inaptness of this epithet in his work is quite obvious. Imitation in this case is so blatant that even Johnston does not deny it, and he admits that the use of this epithet for women is improper. However, he imputes this flagrant imitation to Kālidāsa on the preposterous plea[40] that "the epithets applied by Aśvaghoṣa to women are used of lamps by Kālidāsa, as though he were criticising his predecessor's *hata-tviṣaḥ* as improperly said of women." It is not Kālidāsa's style to imitate any of his predecessors in order to criticise their inapt use of words, whereas Aśvaghoṣa does not hesitate to copy from his predecessors as discussed above.

2. In the *Kumārasambhava* Pārvatī's friend tells Śiva, disguised as a Brahmachārin, that her austerities are meant to achieve the lofty position of union with Śiva, for there is no limit to the reach of ambitions.[41] The last *pāda* of Kālidāsa's verse has been imitated verbatim by Aśvaghoṣa who has incorporated it as the last *pāda* of a verse, describing seductive acts of some women, by substituting the word *pramadānām* for the original word *manorathānām*.[42] Aśvaghoṣa's borrowing in this case is proved by two facts. First, the borrowed *pāda* of the verse (S. VIII, 44) contains eleven syllables, while the rest of the *pādas* of the stanza contain ten syllables each. Secondly, the altered *pāda* meaning "there is no limit to the reach of women" cannot be considered as appropriate as the original one which says: "there is no limit to the reach of ambitions." It is a sheer hyperbole to put women at par with ambitions.
3. Dissuading King Dilīpa from offering his body in exchange for the life of Vasiṣṭha's cow, the lion tells the King in the *Raghuvaṁśa* that he, who wants to give up such prized possessions as universal sovereignty, youth and this lovely body for the sake of a small thing, appears to be thoughtless to him. The second *pāda*[43] of Kālidāsa's said verse has been lifted verbatim and incorporated into the B. by Aśvaghoṣa by simply replacing *kāntam* with *dīptam* in the context where Rājagṛha's King Śreṇya employs the above-mentioned *pāda* in dissuading the Bodhisattva from the path of renunciation as follows:[44] "Since you belong to the great Solar

dynasty and possess *youth and this shining body*, why have you decided to take to mendicancy instead of kingship in utter disregard of the established order?" When the loveliness of body is associated with youth, the use of the epithet *kāntam* "lovely" in respect of *vapus* is quite appropriate as in the *Raghuvaṁśa*, but the adjective *dīptam* "shining" applied by Aśvaghoṣa to the youthful body in this context is inapt. It seems that Aśvaghoṣa has deliberately substituted *dīptam* for *kāntam* in order to glorify the spiritual radiance of the Buddha, but the King who was dissuading the young Prince from renunciation could hardly emphasize the spiritual aspect of his personality in this context.

4. Describing the perplexed condition of Pārvatī held back by smiling Śiva at the time of her going away in anger (*infra*, Chapter III), Kālidāsa (KS. V, 85) says: "Having recognized him (Śiva), trembling, perspiring and bearing her raised foot to step forward, perplexed Pārvatī could neither goforward nor stand there like a mountain stream whose course has been blocked by a rock." Aśvaghoṣa in his S. has copied verbatim not only the last four words of Kālidāsa's said verse but has also borrowed his idea, replacing the simile of a blocked stream by that of a goose swimming on waves.[45] A comparison of these two similes clearly shows the inaptitude of Aśvaghoṣa's simile as a proof of his borrowing the said phrase; for if a goose finds his swimming obstructed by waves in the opposite direction he will not remain stuck up there like a blocked stream but will at once take to his wings; and if he swims in the direction of waves, his speed in swimming will be accelerated by favourable waves. In either case a goose will not remain stranded on waves, like a mountain stream blocked by a rock. So Aśvaghoṣa's simile is inappropriate and exposes his imitation of Kālidāsa's idea and expression.

5. It is said in the *Raghuvaṁśa*[46] that the army at Rāma's behest followed Śatrughna for the success of his mission, just as the preposition *adhi* accompanies the root √i—"to study." This simile of Kālidāsa has been borrowed verbatim by Aśvaghoṣa in the description of Nanda's perturbed mental condition. Nanda who was performing austerities to secure

union with nymphs in heaven was very much perturbed when Ānanda explained to him the transitory nature of the coveted residence in heaven. Aśvaghoṣa says that the said perturbation led to the enhancement of Nanda's final beatitude just as the preposition *adhi* is read by the grammarians with the root √i in a verb.[47] In this connection A. Gawroński observes:[48] "I am still unable to explain this stanza. Anyhow, it cannot be separated from *Raghuvaṁśa* XV, 9. The words *dhātor adhir iva* are common to both verses and cannot be changed in Saundar, as Prof. Hultzsch would like to do." This simile does not appear to be appropriate in the description of Nanda.

6. Describing Umā's beauty during her austerities, Kālidāsa says that her face with the matted locks of hair appeared to be as lovely as with her decorated hair, just as a lotus looks beautiful not only when the rows of bees are sitting on it but also when a (moss-like) *Śaivala* plant is clinging to it.[49] The constituents of this simile of Kālidāsa have been exploited by Aśvaghoṣa in the description of Sundarī's face as follows:[51] "Her face with a beautifying mark on her forehead, with the red lower lip, and with long moving eyes looked lovely like a lotus with a red tip, with bees sitting on it and with a *Śaivala* plant." A *Śaivala* plant does not add to the beauty of a lotus and rather detracts from it. The first member *patita* of the adjectival compound *patita-dvirepham* is redundant and seems to have been added by Aśvaghoṣa only to make up the required number of syllables in the metre. Therefore, Aśvaghoṣa has not succeeded in dovetailing Kālidāsa's apt simile into the said stanza of the S.
7. In Act V of the *Śākuntala* King Duṣyanta speaks of the strains and stresses of kingship, and one of his two panegyrists lauds the King for braving all sorts of hardships for the sake of his people without caring for his own comforts. The idea contained in Kālidāsa's two verses has been expressed by Aśvaghoṣa in different words,[51] but he could not eschew the temptation of copying almost verbatim a phrase from Kālidāsa's work.[52]
8. Kālidāsa's description of the water-sports of King Kuśa

with the women of his harem in the river Sarayū (Ragh. XVI) has been imitated by Aśvaghoṣa with necessary alterations in his B (IV), and there are also some verbatim agreements between the two. It is said in the *Raghuvaṁśa* that King Kuśa, wearing a necklace that was tossed about in waters, enjoyed water-sports in the river with the women, just as a wild elephant, with an uprooted lotus plant sticking to his shoulder, plays with cow-elephants.[53] This description along with its simile has been imitated with some alterations in the B. which says that the Prince surrounded by women wandered in the pleasure-garden, like an elephant accompanied by a herd of cow-elephants in the Himālayan forest.[54] Aśvaghoṣa simplifies the description and replaces Kālidāsa's word *vanyaḥ* by the compound *himavad-vanam* to make up the required number of syllables in the metre, though the word *himavat* has got no special significance here, because the high altitude of the Himalayan forests can hardly be considered suitable for the herds of elephants. Moreover, the word *vanam* is repeated by Aśvaghoṣa.

9. Continuing the aforesaid description, Kālidāsa says (Ragh. XVI, 71) that King Kuśa, bathing in the river Sarayū in the company of beautiful women of his harem, looked like Indra sporting with nymphs in the celestial Gaṅgā. The above-mentioned simile of Indra's sport with nymphs has been imitated almost verbatim in the B.[55]

10. In the description of Siddhārtha's birth (B.I,9 seq.) Aśvaghoṣa imitates, to some extent, Kālidāsa's account of Raghu's birth (Ragh. III, 13 seq.) with some alterations in the wording as well as in the sequence of the original description. Imitating Kālidāsa, Aśvaghoṣa says that like the sun the newly-born Buddha took away the glow of the lamps on account of the resplendent radiance of his limbs[56] (see Note 38); that the Buddha was born for the welfare of the world[57]; that on his birth pleasant and delightful breezes blew,[58] and the fire blazed with gracious flames;[59] and that the King (Śuddhodana), who was delighted at the birth of his son, released all prisoners in his kingdom.[60]

11. In the *Kumārasambhava* (VII, 56-69) Kālidāsa gives a graphic description of the rash movements of eager women who

rushed to the windows of their houses, leaving all other activities, in order to have a glimpse of Śiva who arrived in Himālaya's capital in a procession to marry Pārvatī. The same description with a few alterations has been repeated in the *Raghuvaṁśa* (VII, 5-14) in respect of Aja's procession with Indumatī in the Vidarbha capital for their marriage. Kālidāsa's above-mentioned description of eager women's rash movements has been imitated by Aśvaghoṣa in his *Buddhacharita* (III, 13-24) which describes how women rushed to the windows of their houses to see the Prince after hearing the news that he was going out of the palace for an outing. Although we do not find any verbatim agreement between these two descriptions, yet several ideas in them are strikingly similar. Besides, some ideas and expressions from Canto XVI of the *Raghuvaṁśa* (*supra*, paras 8 & 9) have also been borrowed by Aśvaghoṣa in this description. It is said in the *Raghuvaṁśa* (VII, 5) that the beauties of the town eager to see the couple acted in this manner on the palatial mansions furnished with golden lattice-windows. Similarly Aśvaghoṣa (B. III, 13) says that women went to the upper storey of mansions to see the Prince. According to Kālidāsa,[1] the girdle of a woman, who stood up hurriedly, slipped down on her feet at the time of her rushing forward and only the thread was left in her hand. The same idea has been differently expressed by Aśvaghoṣa (B. III, 14), who says that the movement of the women was obstructed by the slipping down of their girdle-strings. Kālidāsa (Ragh. XVI, 56) says that the flamingoes on the bank of the river Sarayū were frightened by the mutual friction of the armlets of women and by the tinkling of their anklets at the time of their descending into the river along the way of steps. The same idea has been expressed in the B. (III, 15) with the modification that the flocks of birds on the houses were frightened by the jingling of the girdles, by the tinkling of the anklets, and by the clatter of the steps of women on the stairs of palatial mansions. Kālidāsa's description of women, who were unable to carry their own weight on account of the heaviness of their hips and breasts, has been closely imitated by Aśvaghoṣa[62]. Kālidāsa imagines that the windows, packed with eager women's faces fragrant with wine (or with the nectar of the lips), looked as if they (the windows) were adorned with fragrant lotuses having bees in the form of the women's moving eyes.[63] This figurative description of women's faces has also been closely imitated by Aśvaghoṣa who says that the women's lotus-like faces, emerging from the windows and having ear-rings set in motion by each other, looked as if they were lotuses stuck to the mansions[64]. In the *Kumārasambhava* (VII, 65) the ladies looking at Śiva remark that even that woman who may become her slave is blessed and what to say of her who may attain his lap (*supra*, Note 13 of Chapter I). Aśvaghoṣa who expresses this idea in a slightly different manner says[65] that the women, having seen the Prince, murmured low with pure minds and with no other motive: "Blessed is his wife," Aśvaghoṣa's above observation, "with pure minds and with no other motive", seems to be a veiled attack on the above-cited amorous remark of Kālidāsa in the *Kumārasambhava*.

12. Some expressions of Kālidāsa's *Ṛtusaṁhāra* are found copied verbatim in Aśvaghoṣa's works.[66] However, Johnston who denies Kālidāsa the authorship of the *Ṛtusaṁhāra* without any justification sees Aśvaghoṣa's influence on this lyric poem.[67] It is inconceivable that Kālidāsa, the author of an amoristic poem like the *Ṛtusaṁhāra*, would turn for inspiration and phrases to Aśvaghoṣa who is avowedly committed to the propagation of stoical teachings of Buddhism.

The evidence adduced above from the works of the two poets leaves no doubt that Aśvaghoṣa borrowed not only ideas and themes of description but also verbatim passages and phrases from Kālidāsa's works. This conclusion is also corroborated by the fact that on account of the originality of his ideas, expression and style Kālidāsa exercised tremendous influence on the later Sanskrit literature and was acclaimed as Poet Laureate, whereas Aśvaghoṣa whose verbatim borrowing from the earlier works of Sanskrit literature was blatant was simply ignored by the later Sanskrit poets. So there is no substance in the argument advanced by Aśvaghoṣa's supporters that prejudice against Buddhism, a change in taste, and a liking for other methods of writing are responsible for the neglect of his works.

Aśvaghoṣa's blatant verbatim borrowing from Kālidāsa's works indicates that the latter must have flourished at least a century earlier than the former. But we are unable to assign a definite date to Kālidāsa on the basis of his priority to Aśvaghoṣa whose date is far from certain. Although most of the modern scholars are inclined to accept the view, which regards Aśvaghoṣa as a protégé of the Kuṣāṇa King Kaniṣka and places Kaniṣka in the first century A.D., there are several glaring discrepancies between the Buddhist traditions which associate Aśvaghoṣa with Kaniṣka. According to one such tradition, there were six Aśvaghoṣas at different times. Similarly the Buddhist traditions speak of more than one Kaniṣka. According to two stories contained in the *Sūtrālaṅkāra* which is ascribed to Aśvaghoṣa by some ancient authorities, Kaniṣka's reign had already come to an end before the composition of this work. Moreover, the date of the famous King Kaniṣka is also far from certain, and there are serious differences of opinion among scholars about his date. Some scholars who regard Kaniṣka as the founder of the Śaka era (78 A.D.) place him in the first century A.D., while others bring down his date to the fourth century A.D.[68] S. Ch. Vidyabhūṣan assigns Kaniṣka to c. 320 A.D.[69] A majority of modern scholars favour for Kaniṣka a date in the early part of the second century A.D. Anyhow, we cannot determine Aśvaghoṣa's exact date on the basis of his supposed association with Kaniṣka. The lowest limit of Aśvaghoṣa's date is ascertained by the fact that a Chinese translation of *Buddhacharita* is generally assigned to the first quarter of the fifth century A.D. (414-421 A.D.) Moreover, the palaeographical evidence available from the fragments of three Sanskrit plays including the *Śāriputraprakaraṇa* discovered by Lüders at Turfan in Central Asia is also adduced by some scholars to assign Aśvaghoṣa to the second century A.D. On the basis of this palaeographical evidence coupled with the tradition associating him with the Kuṣāṇa King Kaniṣka if Aśvaghoṣa can be assigned to the second century A.D., his literary creditor Kālidāsa must be dated at least a century earlier.

S.N. Dasgupta proposes an early date for Kālidāsa by comparing the law of inheritance alluded to in Act VI of the *Śākuntala* with that laid down in the *Arthaśastra.*[70] According to the principle of inheritance embodied in the *Arthaśāstra* (III, 5), the right of inheritance is restricted to sons, grandsons up to the fourth degree, daughters, brothers, nephews, father, and father's brothers of a dead person; and in the absence of any such inheritor the property of a dead person escheats to the king after making due provision for the maintenance of the deceased's widow and for the performance of his funeral rites. The *Arthaśāstra* does not recognize the right of the dead person's widow to his property. The same law of inheritance depriving a widow of the right of inheriting her husband's property is alluded to in Act. VI of the *Śākuntala* wherein King Duṣyanta's minister recommends to the King that the property of a merchant named Dhanamitra, who died on the sea without leaving any lawful inheritor, should go to the King. However, Duṣyanta orders an enquiry to find out if any widow of the deceased is pregnant, and further decrees, on having been told about the pregnancy of one of the widows, that Dhanamitra's property should go to his prospective child. But in the *Śā kuntala* also the widows of the deceased are not recognized as his inheritors. According to S.N. Dasgupta, the Maurya kings who were greedy changed the Hindu law of inheritance, as recorded in the *Arthaśāstra* in their own interest to grab the property of the people by reducing the number of lawful inheritors. In the opinion of the learned scholar, Kālidāsa, who was in all probability referring to the law of inheritance prevalent in his own days, lived at a time when the Mauryan law of inheritance was in force, because the *Smṛtis* of Manu and Yājñavalkya, which do not recognize such a law of inheritance, include a dead person's widow among his inheritors. On the basis of this evidence S.N. Dasgupta is inclined to place Kālidāsa at a later period of Śungas, and opines[71] that "he may have been either a contemporary of Agnimitra or came shortly after him."

As we have pointed out above, the evidence evailable from the *Mālavikāgnimitra* does not favour the view that Kālidāsa was a contemporary of King Agnimitra. However, the evidence from the said law of inheritance isi mportant and favours an early date for Kālidāsa. It is not possible to assign a definite date to Kālidāsa in the present state of our knowledge of chronological evidence connected with him. However, the cumulative evidence discussed above leads us to the inference that Kālidāsa who is definitely anterior to Aśvaghoṣa may be tentatively placed between 50 B.C. and 50 A.D.

Notes and References

1. A.B. Keith, *A History of Sanskrit Literature*, (reprint, Oxford, 1941) p. 94, remarks : "In this spirited and martial narrative we may justly see the reflex in the poet's mind of Samudragupta's great conquests." However, Prof. V.V. Mirashi on page 34 of his work "*Kālidāsa*" (Bombay, 1969) opines that the *Digvijaya* of Raghu recalls a similar march by Chandragupta II, but on page 65 of the same work he clarifies that the detailed account of Raghu's *Digvijaya* or conquest of the earth is reminiscent of Samudragupta's subjugation of Northern and Southern India and of Chandragupta's conquest of Western India.
2. Keith, *op. cit.*, p. 80; *Sanskrit Drama* (Oxford. 1924), p. 146; Mirashi, *op. cit.*, pp. 34 and 229. But K.G. Sankar (I H.Q. I, p. 316) reads into the *Vikramorvaśīya* the name of the legendary King *Vikramāditya Śakāri* who, in his opinion, gave the name *Vikrama* to "the Saṁvat era of 58 B.C." Thus Sankar uses this very argument to place Kālidāsa in the Ist century B.C.
3. Keith, *A History of Sanskrit Literature*, p. 80; *Sanskrit Drama*, p. 147; Mirashi, *op.cit.*, pp. 34 and 124; Sten Konow, *Festschrift Wackernagel*, 1923, p. 4.
4. Keith, *A History of Sanskrit Literature*, p. 80; *Sanskrit Drama*, p. 147 Mirashi, *op. cit.*, p. 65.
5. *See* V.S. Agrawala's article "Art Evidence in Kālidāsa", *Journal of the U P. Historical Society*, Vol. XXII, Parts 1-2, pp. 81-93; and his book *Gupta Art*, 1947.
6. Keith, *A History of Sanskrit Literature*, p. 76.
7. According to Keith, *op. cit.*, p. 534, the *Jyotirvidābharaṇa* "shows Arabic influence, and need not date before the sixteenth century." S.N. Dasgupta, *A History of Sanskrit Literature*, Vol. I, p. 730, f.n. 1, concurs with Keith. However, Dr Mirashi, *op. cit.*, p. 26, assigns this work to about the twelfth century A.D. and regards the statement contained in it as useless for historical purposes. K.G. Sankar (I.H.Q., I., p. 310) assigns 1242 A.D. to this work on the basis of statements contained in its stanza 30 of Chapter IV.
8. Mbh. II, 25-32.

9. Ibid. XIV, 73-84.
10. R. IV, 40-46.
11. तत्र हूणावरोधानां भर्तृषु व्यक्तविक्रमम् ।
कपोलपाटलादेशि बभूव रघुचेष्टितम् ॥
(Ragh. IV, 68)
12. विनीताध्वश्रमास्तस्य सिन्धुतीरविचेष्टनैः ।
दुधुवुर्वाजिनः स्कन्धाँल्लग्नकुंकुमकेसरान् ॥
(Ragh. IV, 67)
Besides the readings *Sindhu* and *Vankṣū*, the variant *Vankū* is also found in some MSS. The commentator Chāritravardhana explains *Vankū* as a lake in Kashmir. The Mbh. (II, 51, 19-20) says that King Yudhiṣṭhira at his *Rājasūya* sacrifice received a gift of ten thousand famous, fast, trained and giant black-necked asses born on the banks of the river *Vankṣū*.
13. E.B. Cowell, Introduction to the *Buddhacharita* (Oxford, 1893), p. x.
14. *A History of Indian Literature*, Vol. I, p. 490, f.n. 3; cf. *Ibid.* Vol. II, p. 262, f.n. 1.
15. Keith, *A History of Sanskrit Literature*, p. 59; *Cf.* Walter, *Indica*, III, 13; Gawronski, *Studies about the Sanskrit Buddhist Literature*, pp. 27ff.
16. B.I, 43.
17. S.I, 26.
18. B. VIII, 8.
19. Ibid. VIII, 81.
20. (a) बभूव भूमौ पतितो नृपात्मजः शचीपतेः केतुरिवोत्सवक्षये ।
(R. II, 74, 36)
पपात शोकाभिहतो महीपतिः शचीपतेर्वृत्त इवोत्सवे ध्वजः ।
(B. VIII, 73)
(b) घृताच्यां किल संसक्तो दश वर्षाणि लक्ष्मण ।
अहोऽमन्यत धर्मात्मा विश्वामित्रो महामुनिः ॥
(R. IV, 35, 7)
विश्वामित्रो महर्षिश्च विगाढोऽपि महत्तपः ।
दश वर्षाण्यहर्मेने घृताच्याप्सरसा हृतः ॥
(B. IV, 20)
Aśvaghoṣa further improves upon the wording of this verse in the S. VIII, 35.
(c) सुमन्त्रमभियान्तं तं शतशोऽथ सहस्रशः ।
क्व राम इति पृच्छन्तः सूतमभ्यद्रवन्नराः ॥
(R. II, 57, 9)

अथ ब्रुवन्तः समुपेतमन्यवो जनाः पथि च्छन्दकमागताश्रुवः।
क्व राजपुत्रः पुरराष्ट्रनन्दनो हृतस्त्वयासाविति पृष्ठतोऽन्वयुः॥
(B. VIII, 9)

(d) कुरर्य इव दुःखार्ताः
(R. VI, 113,26)

कुररीव दुःखिता
(B. VIII, 51)

21. (a) एष विग्रहवान् धर्मः
(R, I, 21, 10)

धर्मो विग्रहवानिव
(S. II, 56)

(b) देवदुन्दुभयो नेदुः पुष्पवृष्टिश्च खाच्च्युता
(R. I, 18,17)

दिवि दुन्दुभयो नेदुः
(S. II, 54)

पुष्पवर्षं पपात खात्
(S. II, 53)

22. कालः स्वभावो नियतिर्यदृच्छा भूतानि योनिः पुरुष इति चिन्त्या।
संयोग एषां न त्वात्मभावादात्माप्यनीशः सुखदुःखहेतोः॥
(Śvet. Up. I,2)

प्रवृत्तिदुःखस्य च तस्य लोके तृष्णादयो दोषगणा निमित्तम्।
नैवेश्वरो न प्रकृतिर्न कालो नापि स्वभावो न विधिर्यदृच्छा॥
(S. XVI, 17)

Cf. Śvet. Up. V, 2=B. XII, 21.

23. Johnston, Introduction to the English Translation of the *Buddhacharita* (Lahore, 1936), p. xlv.

24. येयं प्रेते विचिकित्सा मनुष्येऽस्तीत्येके नायमस्तीति चैके।
(Kaṭh. Up. I, 20ab)

पुनर्भवोऽस्तीति च केचिदाहुर्नास्तीति केचिन्नियतप्रतिज्ञाः।
एवं यदा संशयितोऽयमर्थस्तस्मात्क्षमं भोक्तुमुपस्थिता श्रीः॥
(B IX, 55),

25. तं स्वाच्छरीरात्प्रवृहेन्मुञ्जादिवेषीकां धैर्येण।
(Kaṭh. Up. II, 3, 17c)

ततो मुञ्जादिषीकेव
(B. XII, 64a)

26. (a) तमो मोहो महामोहस्तामिस्रः क्रोधसंज्ञितः।
(Mbh. XIV, 36, 33ab)

तमो मोहं महामोहं तामिस्रद्वयमेव च।
(B. XII, 33 cd)

(b) प्रोक्तं तद् व्यक्तमित्येव जायते वर्धते च यत् ।
जीर्यते म्रियते चैव चतुर्भिर्लक्षणैर्युतम् ॥
विपरीतमतो यत्तु तदव्यक्तमुदाहृतम् ।

(Mbh. XII, 236, 30. 31 ab)

जायते जीर्यते चैव बध्यते म्रियते च यत् ।
तद्व्यक्तमिति विज्ञेयमव्यक्तं तु विपर्ययात् ॥

(B. XII, 22)

badhyate in this verse seems to be a corrupt reading for *vardhate* which is the correct reading here. One of the MSS. reads *vadhyate*.

(c) य इमां पृथिवीं कृत्स्नामेकच्छत्रां प्रशास्ति ह ।
एक एव स वै राजा पुरमध्यावसत्युत ॥
तत्पुरे चैकमेवास्य गृहं यदधितिष्ठति ।
गृहे शयनमप्येकं निशायां यत्र लीयते ॥

(Mbh. XII, 320, 136-137)

यदा च जित्वापि महीं समग्रां वासाय दृष्टं पुरमेकमेव ।
तत्रापि चैकं भवनं निषेव्यं श्रमः परार्थे ननु राजभावः ॥
राज्ञोऽपि वासोयुगमेकमेव क्षुत्संनिरोधाय तथान्नमात्रा ।
शय्या तथैकासनमेकमेव शेषा विशेषा नृपतेर्मदाय ॥

(B. XI, 47-48)

The use of gerund in *jitvā* (verse 47) is obviously ungrammatical.

(d) कामं पूर्वे धनं मध्ये जघन्ये धर्ममाचरेत् ।

(Mbh. III, 33, 41 ab)

अतश्च यूनः कथयन्ति कामान्मध्यस्य वित्तं स्थविरस्य धर्मम् ।

(B. X, 34 cd)

(e) अभिष्वंगस्तु कामेषु महामोह इति स्मृतः ।
ऋषयो मुनयो देवा मुह्यन्त्यत्र सुखेप्सवः ॥

(Mbh. XIV, 36, 32)

महामोहस्त्वसंमोह काम इत्येव गम्यताम् ।
यस्मादत्र च भूतानि प्रमुह्यन्ति महान्त्यपि ।
तस्मादेष महाबाहो महामोह इति स्मृतः ॥

(B. XII, 34 bc. 35)

(f) त्वं हि सर्वानवद्याङ्गी सर्वाभरणभूषिता ।
विभूषणमिवैतेषां भूषणानामभीप्सितम् ॥

(Mbh I, 170, 37)

विभूषयामास ततः प्रियां स सिषेविषुस्तां न मृजावहार्थम् ।
स्वेनैव रूपेण विभूषिता हि विभूषणानामपि भूषणं सा ॥

(S. IV, 12)

27. Cf. Bh. G. XIII, 1-6 = B. XII, 17-20; Bh. G. V. 10 = S. XIII, 5.

(a) महाभूतान्यहंकारो बुद्धिरव्यक्तमेव च ।

(Bh. G. XIII, 5 ab)

तत्र तु प्रकृतिं नाम विद्धि प्रकृतिकोविद ।
पञ्च भूतान्यहकारं बुद्धिमव्यक्तमेव च ।।

(B. XII, 18)

(b) न चाभावयतः शान्तिरशान्तस्य कुतः सुखम् ।

(Bh. G. II, 66 cd)

अतृप्तौ च कुतः शान्तिरशान्तौ च कुतः सुखम् ।

(S. XI, 33 ab)

(c) इदं शरीरं कौन्तेय क्षेत्रमित्यभिधीयते ।
एतद्यो वेत्ति तं प्राहुः क्षेत्रज्ञ इति तद्विदः ।।

(Bh. G. XIII, 1)

अस्य क्षेत्रस्य विज्ञानात्क्षेत्रज्ञ इति संज्ञि च ।
क्षेत्रज्ञ इति चात्मानं कथयन्त्यात्मचिन्तकाः ।।

(B. XII, 20)

Cf. Mbh XII, 219, 40 for *adhyātma-chintakāḥ*.

(d) अद्वेष्टा सर्वभूतानां मैत्रः करुण एव च ।

(Bh. G. XII, 13 ab)

तस्मात् सर्वेषु भूतेषु मैत्री कारुण्यमेव च ।

(S. XV, 17 ab).

(e) तस्माद्यस्य महाबाहो निगृहीतानि सर्वशः ।
इन्द्रियाणीन्द्रियार्थेभ्यस्तस्य प्रज्ञा प्रतिष्ठिता ।।

(Bh. G. II, 68)

ततः स्मृतिमधिष्ठाय चपलानि स्वभावतः ।
इन्द्रियाणीन्द्रियार्थेभ्यो निवारयितुमर्हसि ।।

(S. XIII, 30)

28. काष्ठादग्निर्जायते मथ्यमानाद् भूमिस्तोयं खन्यमाना ददाति ।
सोत्साहानां नास्त्यसाध्यं नराणां मार्गारब्धाः सर्वयत्नाः फलन्ति ।।

(Pratijñā-Yaugandharāyaṇa I, 17)

काष्ठं हि मथ्नन् लभते हुताशं भूमिं खनन्विन्दति चापि तोयम् ।
निर्बन्धिनः किंचन नास्त्यसाध्यं न्यायेन युक्तं च कृतं च सर्वम् ।।

(B. XIII, 60)

29. S. XVIII, 63-64.

30. Cf. Sukumarsen, (IHQ., 1926), pp. 657 ff., (JASB.), 1930, pp. 181 ff. Prof. Mirashi, *op. cit.*, pp. 14-15, expresses the view that the use of *prāg-eva* supposed to be a peculiar Buddhist expression in Kālidāsa's *Ṛtusaṁhāra* (VI, 23) in the sense of 'how much more' suggests that he lived some time after Buddhist authors began to use Sanskrit for

popularising their religion and hence he must have lived later than Aśvaghoṣa. In this connection, it may be pointed out that some MSS. of the RS. read *prāyeṇa* instead of *prāgeva* which is not explained in the above-mentioned Buddhistic sense by any commentator. Moreover, if this so-called Buddhist expression had stuck to Kālidāsa's mind, he would have repeated its use elsewhere. But no such use of this so-called Buddhist expression can be attested in Kālidāsa's other works. I am unable to agree with Prof. Mirashi's explanation (*op. cit.*, p. 14) that Kālidāsa may have unconsciously used the expression *prāg-eva* in his early work (RS.), but later when he realised that the expression was peculiarly Buddhistic he seems to have avoided it scrupulously. Kālidāsa is too careful an author to use any expression unconsciously. Moreover, if he later became so conscious as to avoid scrupulously the use of even an insignificant Buddhistic expression, he could have hardly thought of borrowing verbatim numerous passages and phrases from Aśvaghoṣa's works as alleged by several modern scholars.

31. For instance, a comparison of *niśvāsa-vātena* (S. IV, 14) with Kālidāsa's expression *niḥśvāsa-bāṣpāgamāt* (Ragh. VII, 68) suggests that *vātena* should be emended as *bāṣpeṇa* or *vāṣpeṇa*. Similarly the phrase *madenāvarjitāḥ* (B IV, 29) which has been translated by Johnston as "pretending to be under the influence of intoxication", can rather be interpreted as "slightly bent down with intoxication" in view of Kālidāsa's use of *āvarjitā* in this sense in the KS. (III, 54)—*āvarjitā kiñchidiva stanābhyām*; Cf. KS. VII, 54; RS. VI, 10 The doubtful reading *Vivasvān* of B. IV, 28 (*infra*, Note 55) can be corrected into the original reading *Marutvān* on the basis of a very similar description in the Ragh. XVI, 71; Cf. Johnston. *op. cit.*, p. 48. Gawroński, Notes on the *Saundarananda*, p. 2, emends *tapo-bhṛṅgaiḥ* of S. (I. 10) as *tapo-mṛgaiḥ* with the help of Ragh. (I, 50).

32. सखा दशरथस्यापि जनकस्य च मन्त्रकृत् ।
संचस्कारोभयप्रीत्या मैथिलेयौ यथाविधि ॥

(Ragh. XV, 31)

स तेषां गोतमश्चक्रे स्ववंशसदृशीः क्रियाः ।

(S.I, 2 ab)

वाल्मीकिरिव धीमांश्च धीमतोः मैथिलेययोः ।

(S.I, 26 cd)

33. See Note 13 for Cowell's views; cf. Johnston, *op. cit.*, p. xvi: "His style proves him to have lived several centuries before Kālidāsa." S.K. De, *A History of Sanskrit Literature*, Vol. I, p. 124, f.n. 2: "To argue that Aśvaghoṣa is later than Kālidāsa is to presume, without sufficient reason, a retrogressive phase in literary evolution." Keith, *A History of Sanskrit Literature*, Preface, p. x., pp. 60 ff.

34. Keith, *op. cit.*, pp. xv-xvi.

35. Johnston, *op. cit.*, p. lxxxvii.

36. Ibid., p xcv.
37. C.W. Gurner, J.A.S.B. (New Series), XXIII, pp. 347 ff.
38. अरिष्टशय्यां परितो विसारिणा सुजन्मनस्तस्य निजेन तेजसा ।
निशीथदीपा सहसा हतत्विषो बभूवुरालेख्यसमर्पिता इव ॥
(Ragh. III, 15)
39. हतत्विषोऽन्याः···श्चासुर्लिखिता इव स्थिताः ।
(B. VIII, 25)
40. Johnston, *op. cit.*, pp. lxxxi-ii.
41. मनोरथानामगतिर्न विद्यते
(KS. V, 64 d); Cf. Vik., p. 45—नास्त्यगतिर्मनोरथानाम् ।
42. प्रमदानामगतिर्न विद्यते
(S. VIII, 44 d)
43. नवं वयः कान्तमिदं वपुश्च
(Ragh. II, 47 b)
44. नवं वयो दीप्तमिदं वपुश्च
(B. X, 23 b)
45. मार्गाचलव्यतिकराकुलितेव सिन्धुः
शैलाधिराजतनया न ययौ न तस्थौ ।
(KS. V, 85 cd)
तं गौरवं बुद्धगतं चकर्ष भार्यानुरागः पुनराचकर्ष ।
सोऽनिश्चयात् नापि ययौ न तस्थौ तरंस्तरंगेष्विव राजहंसः ॥
(S. VIII. 42)
6. रामादेशादनुगता सेना तस्यार्थसिद्धये ।
पश्चादध्ययनार्थस्य धातोरधिरिवाभवत् ॥
(Ragh. XV, 9)
47. बभूव स हि संवेगः श्रेयसस्तस्य वृद्धये ।
धातोरधिरिवाख्याते पठितोऽक्षरचिन्तकैः ॥
(S. XII, 9)
48. A Gawroński, *Notes on the Saundarananda* (II series, 1922), p. 31.
49. यथा प्रसिद्धैर्मधुरं शिरोरुहैर्जटाभिरप्येवमभून्तदाननम् ।
न षट्पदश्रेणिभिरेव पंकजं सशैवलासंगमपि प्रकाशते ॥
(KS. V, 9)
50. तस्या मुखं तत्सतमालपत्रं ताम्राधरोष्ठं चिकुरायताक्षम् ।
रक्ताधिकाग्रं पतितद्विरेफं सशैवलं पद्ममिवाबभासे ॥
(S. IV, 21)
51. Śāk. V, 6-7=B. XI, 45-46.
52 स्वसुखनिरभिलाषः खिद्यसे लोकहेतोः ।
(Śāk. V, 7 a).
आसंगकाष्ठप्रतिमो हि राजा लोकस्य हेतोः परिखेदमेति ।
(B. XI, 45 cd)

53. स नौविमानादवतीर्य रेमे विलोलहारः सह ताभिरप्सु ।
स्कन्धावलग्नोद्धृतपद्मिनीकः करेणुभिर्वन्य इव द्विपेन्द्रः ।।

(Ragh. XVI, 68)

54. अथ नारीजनवृतः कुमारो व्यचरद् वनम् ।
वासितायूथसहितः करीव हिमवद्वनम् ।।

(B. IV, 27)

55. आकाशगंगारतिरप्सरोभिर्वृतो मरुत्वाननुयातलीलः ।

(Ragh. XVI, 71 cd)

आक्रीड इव विभ्राजे विवस्वानप्सरोवृतः

(B. IV, 28 cd)

The reading *Vivasvān* should be corrected as *Marutvān* (*supra*, Note 31); *cf.* Johnston's note on its text and translation. Similarly the doubtful reading *vibhrāje* could be corrected as *babhrāje* (3rd person singular perfect of √*bhrāj*—"to shine") which would solve the problem of interpretation discussed by Johnston, *op. cit.*

56. स हि स्वगात्रप्रभयोज्ज्वलन्त्या दीपप्रभां भास्करवन्मुमोष ।

(B. I, 13 ab)
Cf. Note 38 & 39,

57. भवो हि लोकाभ्युदयाय तादृशाम् ।

(Ragh. III, 14 d)

बोधाय जातोऽस्मि जगद्धितार्थमन्त्यां भवोत्पत्तिरियं ममेति ।

(B. I, 15 ab)

58. दिशः प्रसेदुर्मरुतो ववुः सुखाः

(Ragh. III, 14 a)

वाता ववुः स्पर्शसुखा मनोज्ञाः

(B. I, 22a)

59. प्रदक्षिणार्चिर्हविरग्निराददे

(Ragh. III, 14 b)

जज्वाल सौम्यार्चिरनीरितोऽग्निः

(B. I, 22d)

60. न संयतस्तस्य बभूव रक्षितुर्विसर्जयेद् यं सुतजन्महर्षितः ।

(Ragh. 20 ab)

नरपतिरपि पुत्रजन्मतुष्टो विषयगतानि विमुच्य बन्धनानि ।

(B. I, 82 ab)

61. KS. VII, 61; Ragh. VII, 10.

62. एता गुरुश्रोणिपयोधरत्वादात्मानमुद्वोढुमशक्नुवत्यः ।

(Ragh. XVI, 60 ab)

कासांचिदासां तु वरांगनानां जातत्वराणामपि सोत्सुकानाम् ।
गतिं गुरुत्वाज्जगृहुर्विशालाः श्रोणीरथाः पीनपयोधराश्च ।।

(B. III, 16)

63. तासां मुखैरासवगन्धगर्भैर्व्याप्तान्तराः सान्द्रकुतूहलानाम् ।
विलोलनेत्रभ्रमरैर्गवाक्षाः सहस्रपत्राभरणा इवासन् ॥
(KS. VII, 62; Ragh. VII, II)

64. वातायनेभ्यस्तु विनिःसृतानि परस्परायासितकुण्डलानि ।
स्त्रीणां विरेजुर्मुखपंकजानि सक्तानि हर्म्येष्विव पंकजानि ॥
(B. III, 19)

65. धन्यास्य भार्येति शनैरवोचन्
शुद्धैर्मनोभिः खलु नान्यभावात् ।
(B. III, 23 cd)

66. शरादिकादम्बविघट्टितानि
(RS. IV, 6 b)
पद्मानि कादम्बविघट्टितानि
(S.X, 38 d)

(b) कारण्डवाननविघट्टितवीचिमालाः
(RS. III, 8a)
स्थितकारण्डवघट्टितं चकाशे
(B. V, 53 d)

(c) कठिनः स्तनेषु जघनेषु पीनः
(RS. VI, 10)
कठिनैः पस्पृशुः पीनैः संहतैर्वल्गुभिः स्तनैः ।
(B. IV, 29 cd)

67. Johnston, *op. cit.*, p. lxxxi.
68. See Appendix V (pp. 611-614) of *A History of Indian Literature*, Vol, II, by M. Winternitz, for divergent views on the date of Kaniṣka.
69. Proceedings and Transactions of the First Oriental Conference, Poona, 1919, I, pp. xxxiii ff.
70. S.N. Dasgupta, *A History of Sanskrit Literature*, pp. 732 ff.
71. Ibid., p. 735.

3

The Poetic Art of Kālidāsa

Kālidāsa is undoubtedly the greatest Sanskrit poet whose poetic art marked by polish and perfection serves as a model for the later Sanskrit poets. It cannot be gainsaid that Kālidāsa's artistic genius is chiefly responsible for the finish and supremacy of his poetic art, but his learning and milieu must have also contributed in no small measure to its development. Therefore, his poetic art cannot be fully appreciated in isolation and should be viewed in proper perspective.

Kālidāsa who was highly learned in various branches of knowledge as noted above (Chapter I) must have fully acquainted himself with the earlier poetic works and must have naturally aspired to excel them. It is a well-known fact that the *Rāmāyaṇa* of Vālmīki, who is styled as the *first poet*[1] in regard to the composition of ornate poetry, blazes a new trail in the realm of Sanskrit literature and presents a new model of poetry which attaches greater importance to the employment of similes and metaphors and to the delineation of natural scenery and human sentiments than to a simple narration of events. Aśvaghoṣa's priority to Kālidāsa, suggested by several modern scholars, has been already disproved by us in Chapter II above; and no other important poet preceding Kālidāsa is known to us at present. It would be gratuitous to assume that there was no poetic activity in the period intervening between Vālmīki and Kālidāsa. But all the poets of the intervening period were so mediocre that they did not merit any mention by Kālidāsa who does not hesitate to name his illustrious predecessors in the realm of drama. In the estimate of Kālidāsa Vālmīki is his only worthy predecessor whose immortal Epic affords inspiration and illumination to later poets. In the beginning of the

Raghuvaṁśa (I, 4) Kālidāsa expresses his gratitude to the earlier poets (i.e., Vālmīki etc.) for facilitating his task of describing the Solar dynasty (*Sūrya-vaṁśa*) through their previous description of the same; and eleswhere in the *Raghuvaṁśa* (XV, 32-41) Kālidāsa reverentially refers to Vālmīki as *ādya kavi*, and describes his work as a new (first) path (style) of the poet (*kavi-prathama-paddhatim*). Although Kālidāsa excels Vālmīki in some respects, yet it must be ungrudgingly conceded that the former is greatly indebted to the latter who still remains unsurpassed in certain poetic descriptions. Many themes, expressions and similes of Kālidāsa are easily traceable to the *Rāmāyaṇa*. For instance, in the *Raghuvaṁśa* (XIV, 68) Kālidāsa employs Vālmīki's favourite simile[5]: *cakranda vignā kurarīva bhūyaḥ* "agitated Sītā cried aloud like a female osprey (*Kurarī*)".

Kālidāsa who is renowned as a poet of beauty, harmony and perfection creates enchanting word-pictures and expresses human feelings with poise and restraint. In his flight of poetic imagination Kālidāsa conceives of only the beautiful, refined and harmonious aspects of life and Nature. Kālidāsa's poetry, which reveals his keen observation of Nature and deep insight into human sentiments, is charming and thought-provoking. His poetic art, which is distinguished by elegance, accomplishment, and harmony of sound and sense, delights our mind and elevates our soul.

We shall make below a brief estimate of his poetic art revealed in his lyrics and epics.

The Ṛtusaṁhāra

The authenticity of the *Ṛtusaṁhāra* as Kālidāsa's composition has been doubted by some scholars on the grounds that it is inferior to the other works of the poet in poetic merit; that it has not been commented upon by Mallinātha who has written commentaries on the other three poems of Kālidāsa; and that it has not been cited by Sanskrit rhetoricians. However, this doubt is unwarranted, because Vatsabhaṭṭi, who in his Mandasor inscription imitates the *Meghadūta*, borrows expressions from the *Ṛtusaṁhāra* also and adapts in a single verse (31) the idea contained in two verses (V, 2-3) of the *Ṛtusaṁhāra*. Besides, two verses (VI, 17. 20) of the *Ṛtusaṁhāra* included in the *Subhāṣitāvali* have been attributed by Vallabhadeva to Kālidāsa.

The title *Ṛtusaṁhāra* which literally means "A Collection of Seasons" has been, in fact, employed by the poet to signify "A Collection of Descriptions of Seasons as viewed by a lover." This is evident from the very first stanza of the poem, which is addressed by the poet to his beloved sweet-heart who is again addressed in the same way in several other stanzas of the poem. So the *Ṛtusaṁhāra* does not contain a mere matter-of-fact description of Nature in various seasons, but it paints miniature pictures of beautiful young ladies in the natural setting of different seasons. The poet's keen observation of various phases of Nature can be seen at its best in this poem where he brings out the beauties of natural environments in which so many different aspects of voluptuous beauty are graphically depicted and amorous acts and feelings of lovers are vividly delineated.

The *Ṛtusaṁhāra*, which consists of six Cantos containing the description of six Indian seasons,[3] viz., Summer, rainy season, Autumn, cool season (*Hemanta*), Winter (*Śiśira*), and *Spring, opens with an account of summer and* closes with that of Spring, which is the first season of the year. With a view to making the last Canto of his poem most delightful and charming, Kālidāsa seems to have deliberately placed the description of Spring at the end of the Collection of Seasons. In the first Canto the poet describes both oppressive and delightful aspects of Summer. Days are very hot, but nights are pleasant. Due to the debilitating effect of burning heat animals hostile to each other by nature stay together tamely. For instance, a serpent takes shelter under a peacock, and a frog under the hood of a snake; and the devastating forest fire compels wild beasts such as elephants and lions to give up their natural hostility and to seek common shelter in a river. In a few stanzas devoted to the pleasant aspects of Summer the poet describes the nocturnal delight of young lovers enjoying song, dance and wine in moonlight on the terraces of palatial buildings. He gives an attractive account of fine dresses and decorations of young ladies in Summer. The poet imagines that the moon, which has eagerly beheld for long at night the charming faces of sleeping beauties in white mansions, has turned pale due to abashment at day-break.

The advent of the rainy season is heralded by the appearance of dark drizzling clouds accompanied by lightning and thunder. Here Kālidāsa likens a dark cloud to an elephant, lightning to a banner, and thunder to a drum announcing the advent of the rainy season. In the following stanzas the poet vividly describes the overcast sky, gushing rivers, green trees, beautiful flowers, fluttering birds, peacock-dance, and forests teeming with lotus-eyed gazelles. The natural scenes of rainy season evoke the emotion of love in the hearts of lovers and torment the minds of separated lovers. Love-stricken women go to meet their lovers in the rainy nights, darkened by thundering clouds, on the paths illuminated by lightning. Maidens adorn themselves with the garlands made of different kinds of seasonal flowers. Clouds laden with water gladden their lofty resort, the Vindhya mountain, parched by Summer.

The poet metaphorically describes Autumn as a newly-wedded lovely bride having white *Kāśa* flowers as her upper garment, blooming lotuses as her beautiful face, the notes of exultant flamingoes as the tinkling of her anklets, and partly ripe paddy as her pretty slender body. In this season Nature has put on a white garb : now nights look white with moonlight; the waters of rivers appear white with flamingoes; lakes are white with white water-lilies; forests present a white spectacle with *Sapta-parṇa* trees bent down with the burden of flowers; gardens are white with jasmine flowers; and the earth appears white with *Kāśa* flowers.[4] Discerning feminine beauty in Nature, the poet imagines that the lovely gait of maidens has been captured by flamingoes, the beauty of maidens' faces by full-blown lotuses, the enchanting glances of maidens by blue lotuses, and the fascinating sportive movements of the eye-brows of maidens by ripples of water. Continuing in the same strain, Kālidāsa imagines that green creepers laden with flowers capture the beauty of maidens' arms decorated with ornaments; and that the jasmine radiant with the crimson Aśoka flowers excels in beauty the shining teeth and red lips of smiling maidens.

The fourth Canto which describes *Hemanta* contains a fewer number of stanzas (18) in comparison with the preceding three

Cantos, as the first and the second Canto consist of 28 verses each while there are 26 verses in the third Canto. The advent of *Hemanta* presents a fascinating natural scenery with blooming *Lodhra* trees and with fields of fully ripe paddy and newly-sprouted barley crops. Now lotuses have faded and the earth is covered with frost in the morning. Lakes look charming with clear waters, exulting flamingoes, and full-blown blue lotuses. In this season maidens discard fine silken garments, bracelets, girdles and anklets, and anoint their bodies with the paste of a fragrant wood (*Kālīyaka*), decorate their faces by painting lines or figures on them with fragrant and coloured substances such as musk, saffron, etc., and scent their tresses with the smoke of black Aloe wood.

The fifth Canto which describes Winter (*Śiśira*) is very short consisting of only sixteen verses. In this season people keep the windows of their houses closed and enjoy fire, sun-shine, heavy raiments and pleasures of youth. No one likes cool sandal-paste, open terrace and chilly winds in this season. Some stanzas of this Canto contain a lascivious description of amorous sports of young lovers.

In the opening verse of the last Canto the poet metaphorically describes Spring as a warrior equipped with sharp arrows in the form of blossoms of blooming mango trees, and with a bow-string in the form of a row of black bees to pierce the hearts of love-stricken lovers. Trees are now laden with flowers, waters are dotted with lotuses, maidens are full of youthful passion, breeze is fragrant, evenings are enjoyable, and days are pleasant. Thus everything is delightful in Spring. Fresh *Karṇikāra* flowers fixed on the ears of maidens, and red *Aśoka* flowers and full-blown jasmine flowers tucked to their flowing black tresses enhance the beauty of lovely maidens. Ladies adorn themselves with pearl necklaces, girdles, bracelets, anklets and sandal-paste, and put on fine garments dyed with saffron. The poet imagines that not only young men and women but other creatures are also charged with amorous passion generated by Spring. So the passionate male cuckoo intoxicated with the drink of mango-juice kisses his mate, and the humming black bee perched on a lotus makes blandishments to its beloved. The enchanting beauty of Nature enraptures the mind of everyone. Lovely gardens resplendent with jasmine (*Kunda*) flowers, which are white like the amorous laughter of a bride, tempt the passion-free mind of even an ascetic, not to speak of the passionate minds of young people. The poet concludes his poem with the benediction that happiness may be bestowed on you by the world-conquering god Cupid who is accompanied by Spring, whose arrow is a cluster of mango blossoms, whose bow is a *Kiṁśuka* flower, whose bow-string is a row of black bees, whose spotless white umbrella is the moon, whose exultant elephant is the fragrant breeze blowing from the *Malaya* mountain, and whose bards are cuckoos.

Although the *Rāmāyaṇa* contains vivid descriptions of some seasons, such as Autumn and rainy season, and Vālmīki's influence is discernible on Kālidāsa in the description of rainy season,[5] yet Kālidāsa's description of seasons from a lover's viewpoint is entirely original.

The Meghadūta

The *Meghadūta*, which contains nearly 120 stanzas[6] composed in the *Mandākrāntā* metre of four lines of seventeen syllables each, shows Kālidāsa's poetic art at its best. The poem is divided into two parts, called *Pūrvamegha* and *Uttaramegha*.

The opening stanza of the *Meghadūta* describes the sad plight of a separated lover (*Yakṣa*), who as a punishment for the negligence of his duty was banished by his master (*Kubera*) for a period of twelve months, and who made his temporary stay in a hermitage on the mount *Rāmagiri*[7] where waters were hallowed by Sītā's ablutions. Continuing the description in the following verses, the poet says that after the expiry of eight months on the first day of the month of *Āṣāḍha* when the *Yakṣa* saw a dark cloud looking like an elephant on the peak of the mountain, he became pensive and felt the pangs of separation. In order to ensure his dear wife's life threatened by the agony of separation aggravated by the approach of the rainy season, the *Yakṣa* desired to convey to her the message of his own welfare through the cloud. Therefore, he greeted the cloud with *Kuṭaja* flowers and flattering words, and begged it to go to the city of *Alakā* and to convey his message to his beloved wife whom the Cloud-messenger would find absorbed in counting the remaining days of his exile; for, in separation the bond of hope sustains women's flower-like, loving and tender heart which is susceptible to instant fall. Then the *Yakṣa* told the Cloud-messenger the way to his hometown *Alakā*.

In the context of guiding the Cloud on its northward journey to the *Yakṣa's* home the poet not only displays his knowledge of important regions, rivers, mountains and cities of northern India but also portrays a vivid picture of the landscape to be surveyed by the Cloud-messenger during its aerial journey. Besides, Kālidāsa imparts wherever possible a touch of enchanting feminine beauty to the lovely description of natural scenery on the suggested path from Mount *Rāmagirī* to *Alakā*. The Cloud-messenger is asked by the *Yakṣa* to fly over *Māla* plateau, Mount *Āmrakūṭa*, the river *Revā* (*Narmadā*) at the foot of the *Vindhya* mountain, the *Daśārṇa* country (named after the river *Daśārṇā* modern *Dasān*, an affluent of the Betwā) with its capital city *Vidiśā*, and to enjoy the waters of the river *Vetravatī* (*Betwā*) and then to take rest at the *Nīchairgiri* (*Udayagiri*) mountain where the caves, giving out the odour of amorous sports of courtesans, betoken the youthful passion of citizens. After having rested there for a while, the Cloud will proceed further to sprinkle with light showers the jasmine-gardens on the banks of the *Vananadī*[8] (v.l. *Naganadī*), and to have a glimpse of the faces of flower-plucking maidens whose lotuses fixed on the ears have faded due to the frequent wiping off of sweat from their cheeks. The *Yakṣa* implores the Cloud-messenger not to miss Ujjayanī, the city of palatial mansions and beautiful maidens, even though the Cloud has to make a detour in its northward route. On its way to Ujjayinī the Cloud will enjoy the delightful scenery of the rivers *Nirvindhyā* and *Sindhu*.[9] The poet devotes about a dozen stanzas to the description of his favourite city Ujjayinī as discussed above in Chapter I. The Cloud-messenger is particularly urged to visit at Ujjayinī the holy temple of *Mahākāla* in the evening. The *Yakṣa* requests the Cloud to proceed on its journey after a night's stay at Ujjayinī, to cross the river *Gambhīrā*, to worship the god *Skanda* in the temple on the *Devagiri* hill, to fly over the river *Charmaṇvatī* (*Chambal*) and

Daśapura (*Mandasor*), and to reach the *Brahmāvarta* country where Arjuna displayed his bravery in the battlefield of *Kurukṣetra*. The Cloud is then asked to purify itself in the waters of the sacred river *Sarasvatī*, to proceed from there to the river *Gaṅgā* in the vicinity of *Kanakhala*[10] and then to go northward through the *Krauñcha* pass to Mount *Kailāsa* which serves as a mirror for celestial ladies and which rising high in the sky with white peaks looking like water-lilies stands majestically as if it were a huge mass of Śiva's loud laughter piled up day after day. The *Yakṣa* tells the Cloud that it would enjoy at the foot of Mount *Kailāsa* the waters of the lake *Mānasa* abounding in golden lotuses; and that it would not fail to recognize at the first sight the city of *Alakā* situated in the lap (on the higher level) of *Kailāsa*; for, the city with its palatial mansions, with the river *Gaṅgā* flowing nearby and with raining clouds hovering over it, looks in the rainy season like a lovely maiden in her lover's lap with her white silken garment slipping down and with her hair decorated with a string of pearls.

In the second half (*Uttaramegha*) of the poem Kālidāsa gives the reins to his imagination in the description of *Alakā*, the *Yakṣa's* home, and his separated wife. *Alakā* is portrayed as a fairyland having palatial mansions, all sorts of gems, sweet music, ever-blossoming trees, and amorous sports of beautiful maidens. Describing his own home situated to the north of Kubera's palace, the *Yakṣa* tells the Cloud-Messenger that his home can be recognized from a distance through its beautiful archway looking like a rain-bow; that in his garden there is a coral tree reared by his wife; that there is also a well which has a flight of steps paved with emeralds; and that in that well golden lotuses grow and swans swim without thinking of the lake *Mānasa*. Then the *Yakṣa* paints a beautiful but pathetic picture of his wife who is a paragon of beauty but emaciated and sorrowful due to separation. The Cloud is requested by the *Yakṣa* to approach his house gently without disturbing his wife's happy dream of union with him and to convey his message to her when she is awake. In his message the *Yakṣa* assures his wife of his own welfare, of his constant love for her, and of the certainty of their happy reunion after four months. In the end *Yakṣa* bids farewell to the Cloud-Messenger with the prayer that after doing this favour to him out of amity or compassion the Cloud may go wherever it likes and may never be separated even for a moment from its beloved lightning.

The motif of sending a message to a separated lover seems to have been borrowed by Kālidāsa from the *Rāmāyaṇa* as pointed out by Mallināth in his commentary on the first stanza of the poem.[11] The internal evidence from the Megh. corroborates the view that Kālidāsa has drawn inspiration from the *Rāmāyaṇa* for this lyrical poem. In the opening verse of the poem Kālidāsa refers to the *Rāmagiri Āśrama* hallowed by Sītā, and in verse 37 of the *Uttaramegha* he compares the Cloud-Messenger to *Hanumat* and the Yakṣa's wife to Sītā. There is no doubt that Kālidāsa, who made a deep study of the *Rāmāyaṇa*, was naturally influenced by it. However, the entire concept of the Megh. as well as its poetic beauty is Kālidāsa's original contribution which has originated a new *genre* in Sanskrit Literature. In this poem Kālidāsa has not only portrayed the word-pictures of natural scenery in vivid details but has also invested them with human feelings—especially with erotic sentiment. Kālidāsa's restrained and graphic delineation of the agony, anguish, frustration and hopes of separated lovers stands no comparison and remains unsurpassed. The poet's keen observation of Nature, extraordinary power of imagination, penetrating insight into the human mind, maturity of thought, and choice of apt expression are fully illustrated in the Megh. which is undoubtedly his masterpiece. Although some scholars surmise that Kālidāsa's personal experience of suffering in separation from his beloved is reflected in the poem, yet it is not so much his personal experience as his superb poetic art which has created this lyrical gem of Sanskrit literature.

The Kumārasambhava

The *Kumārasambhava* which ranks among the five important *Mahākāvyas* of Sanskrit, namely, the *Raghuvaṃśa*, the *Kumārasambhava*, the *Kirātārjunīya*, the *Śiśupālavadha* and the

Naiṣadhacharita, is regarded by most of the modern scholars as earlier than the *Raghuvaṃśa* as pointed out above. Although the *Kumārasambhava* at present contains seventeen Cantos, only the first eight Cantos commented upon by Mallinātha and Aruṇagirinātha are considered to be Kālidāsa's genuine composition and the remaining nine Cantos seem to have been added later on with a view to bringing the story of the epic to a fruitful conclusion relating to the destruction of the demon Tāraka at the hands of the god *Kumāra* whose birth (*sambhava*) forms the theme of the poem. The spurious character of Cantos IX-XVII of the *Kumārasambhava* is fully exposed by the inferiority of their poetic qualities in respect of ideas, expression, metre and style.

A popular mythological legend,[12] pertaining to the birth of the god Kumāra (*Kārttikeya*), has been suitably adapted by Kālidāsa to form the theme of his *Mahākāvya*. Some scholars surmise (see Note 3 of Chapter II) that Kālidāsa might have composed the epic *Kumārasambhava* to celebrate the birth of Kumāragupta, the son of Chandragupta II. Even if it is conceded, for the sake of argument, that Kālidāsa flourished during the reign of Chandragupta II, the tenor of the epic lends no support to the conjecture that it could have been even remotely connected with the celebration of the birth of a prince. The theme of the epic is obviously concerned with the poet's personal faith, for he pays obeisance to Śiva in the opening stanzas of the *Śākuntala*, the *Mālavikāgnimitra* and the *Vikramorvaśīya*, and to both Śiva and Pārvatī in the first verse of the *Raghuvaṃśa*. Kālidāsa's poetic genius has fashioned a simple mythological theme into an unsurpassed epic poem of exceptional merit.

The poem opens with a grand description of the Himālayas. The poet imagines the imposing northern mountain range as possessed of a divine soul, and figuratively describes it as the lord of mountains and earth's measuring rod with its extremities submerged into the eastern and western oceans. The Himālayas are depicted by Kālidāsa as the source of all sorts of gems, metals, trees, herbs and flowers, and as the abode of the Siddhas, demigods, beautiful Vidyādhara maidens, horse-faced Kinnara women, Yakṣas and Kirātas. The poet imagines that snow in no way detracts from the grandeur of the

Himālayas; that certain fluorescent herbs serve as oil-less lamps at night for the amorous sports of foresters and their wives in the Himalayan caves; and that the mountain range affords shelter in its caves to darkness hidden there due to the fear of the sun. Then Kālidāsa describes the marriage of Himālaya with Menā and the birth of their son *Maināka* and daughter *Pārvatī* alias *Umā*, and devotes over two dozen stanzas to the charming description of gradual growth of Pārvatī from a sweet and loving child into a lovely maiden. Himālaya was both purified and adorned by her birth, just as a lamp by a bright flame, the path of heaven by the celestial river Gaṅgā, and a scholar by correct speech. Entire learning acquired in the previous birth automatically came to intelligent Pārvatī at the time of instruction in the same way as the flights of flamingoes come to the river Gaṅgā in Autumn, and just as glow returns to a fluorescent herb (Mahauṣadhi) at night. The beauty of her form, looking pretty with perfect and proportionate limbs, was fully displayed by youth, just as a painting is made life-like by the touch of a brush, and a lotus is opened up by the rays of the sun. After giving a graphic description of various aspects of her youthful beauty, the poet concludes that the Creator created her with great effort by appropriately apportioning to her limbs the beauty of all the natural standards of comparison with a view to beholding entire beauty amassed in a single form, as it were.

One day Nārada visited Himālaya, saw Pārvatī near her father and predicted that she would marry Śiva. On hearing this prediction Himālaya directed Pārvatī, accompanied by her two friends, to serve Śiva who was then engaged in meditation on a mountain-peak. Accordingly Pārvatī approached Śiva and sought his permission to serve him. Although she was an impediment to Śiva's meditation, he consented to her service. So she began to serve him by plucking flowers for worship, by sweeping sacrificial altar, by fetching water, and by bringing sacrificial grass.

The second Canto describes the distress of the gods who approached the Creator (*Brahman*) to save them from the oppressive might of the demon Tāraka. The Creator expressed his inability to help them and advised them to allure Śiva's restrained and tranquil mind to Umā's beauty, because a son born out of the union of Śiva and Umā would destroy Tāraka and rid the gods of their miseries. Then Indra sought the help of Kāma (Cupid) to achieve the gods' desired object.

The third Canto contains a brilliant description of the enticing efforts of Kāma to produce amorous passion in Śiva's mind for Pārvatī. Accompanied by Spring, Kāma went with his wife Rati to the vicinity of Śiva's hermitage on the Himālayas. With the advent of Spring there was new life all around. Flowers bloomed on the *Aśoka* trees. New sprouts and flowers appeared on the mango trees. Birds were chirping merrily, bees were humming and gentle fragrant breeze was blowing. Spring filled Nature with amatory passion. Consequently the bee drank honey with its beloved in the same flower-cup; the doe with her eyes closed was rubbed gently by the black antelope with his horn; and the trees were in close embrace with creepers. In the midst of these enchanting surroundings when Kāma saw Śiva unaffected and firm in his deep meditation, fear and despair gripped Kāma to such an extent that he failed to notice his bow and arrow slipping from his hands. However, he summoned up courage when he saw beautiful and charming Umā enter the threshold of Śiva's hermitage . At that time Śiva withdrew from his meditation and allowed Umā's entry into his hermitage. She scattered flowers at Śiva's feet and paid obeisance to him with her bowed head. Śiva blessed her to get a husband who would never think of another woman. Kāma deemed it to be an opportune moment to achieve his object. When Umā was offering a rosary of seeds of Gangetic lotuses to Śiva and he was going to accept it, Kāma aimed his unfailing and enticing arrow at Śiva who felt a bit excited and cast his glance at Umā's beautiful face charming with the *Bimba*-like lower lip. But Śiva soon controlled his passion and looked around to find out the cause of his excitement. He spotted Kāma ready to discharge his arrow at Śiva. A dazzling fire with high flames suddenly issued forth from the third eye of enraged Śiva and reduced Kāma to ashes before the gods' voices, beseeching Śiva to withhold his anger, could reach him. On Kāma's destruction his wife Rati became unconscious; Śiva vanished from the scene; and Umā, finding her father's ambition frustrated and her own beauty unavailing, returned home in utter humiliation and despair.

The fourth Canto depicts a touching scene of Rati's pathetic lamentation over the death of her husband. It is a brilliant illustration of the aesthetic sentiment of pathos. On regaining consciousness, Rati burst into a heart-rending lamentation. Having sighted only the ashes of her husband, she fell down on the ground and wailed, with her hair dishevelled, so piteously that she made the entire forest pathetic like herself. When her husband's friend Spring came to console her, she wept more bitterly beating her breast, because grief becomes more intense on the sight of one's near and dear ones. She begged Spring to prepare a funeral pyre for her in order to unite her with her dead husband; for, the moonlight goes with the moon and the lightning vanishes with the cloud, and thus even inanimate objects show that women should follow the path of their husbands. She again requested Spring to offer, after her death, a single handful of water in performance of the joint obsequies of both of them, because in the other world also Kāma would drink that single water-offering with her without dividing it into two. When Rati was about to end her life, a heavenly voice dissuaded her from committing suicide by assuring her that she would again be united with Kāma when Śiva married Pārvatī.

The fifth Canto describes how Pārvatī, who had realised the futility of her physical charm to win Śiva, won him ultimately through her austerities and devotion. Umā, whom her mother had previously tried unsuccessfully to dissuade from undertaking severe austerities, went to the mountain-peak called *Gaurī-śikhara* (so named after her) to perform austerities with the consent of her father. She discarded all her precious ornaments, embellishments and fine garments and put on a dress of bark. She sat and slept on bare ground. In Summer she sat in the midst of four burning fires and gazed at the sun. In the rainy season she slept at night in the open on a rock, exposing herself to squalling winds and rain. In Winter she stood in cold water lashed by snowy winds. Thus she excelled even ascetics in her austerities. Although Śiva was pleased with her rigorous austerities, he appeared before her in the garb of a young Brahmachārin (Vedic student) to test the sincerity of her love. When he enquired from Umā the purpose of her austerities, her female companion told him that Umā was performing austerities to obtain Lord Śiva as her husband. On hearing this reply, the Brahmachārin expressed his surprise and asked Umā whether she was aware that Śiva puts on an elephant-skin dripping with blood, wears bracelets of serpents on his hands, resides in cemeteries, is deformed in appearance with a third eye, rides on an old bull, and is of unknown extraction. He again put the question whether Śiva possesses any of the qualities of a bridegroom to be worthy of Umā. The Brahmachārin's uncharitable remarks about Śiva angered Pārvatī who rebuked the Brahmachārin for his ignorance about the greatness of Śiva. She lauded Mahādeva and asserted her unwavering love for Śiva. When the Brahmachārin was about to say something more, she quipped angrily: "Not only he, who speaks ill of the great, commits a sin but he also, who listens to him, is a sinner; or I shall rather go away from here". Then as soon as she began to walk away, Śiva revealed his identity and smilingly held her back. Having recognized him, trembling, perspiring and bearing her raised foot to step forward, perplexed Pārvatī could neither go forward nor stand there like a mountain stream whose course has been blocked by a rock. Then Śiva said to her: "O fair-limbed lady ! I am henceforth your slave purchased with your austerities."

In the sixth Canto Kālidāsa dwells upon the procedure followed by Śiva in securing Himālaya's consent for the hand of Pārvatī. After Śiva had expressed his desire to marry Umā, she conveyed her wish through a friend to him that her father (Himālaya) should be formally approached for her hand. Śiva then thought of the Seven celestial Seers who together with Arundhatī appeared before him and went on his behalf to Himālaya as wooers to seek the hand of Pārvatī for Śiva. With the concurrence of his wife Himālaya gladly agreed to give away his daughter in marriage to Śiva, and their wedding was fixed on the fourth ensuing day. In this Canto Kālidāsa gives the reins to his imagination to describe the lustre of the Seven celestial Seers, their advent to Śiva on Mount Kailāsa, the grandeur of the Himālayas on the arrival of the Seven celestial Seers in the Himālayan Capital named *Oṣadhiprastha*, and the shyness of Pārvatī at the time of the Seven celestial Seers' proposal to Himālaya about her marriage with Śiva. She is depicted as standing by the side of her father, with her eyes downcast, counting the petals of the lotus held in her hand.

The seventh Canto contains a graphic description of the wedding. The capital of Himālaya wore a festive look with flowers strewn in streets, and with festoons and silken banners fluttering everywhere. Pārvatī was lavishly adorned for the wedding. When the bridegroom Śiva arrived in a procession accompanied by the gods, goddesses, sages and his attendants, the ladies of the city rushed in haste to the windows of their houses to have a glimpse of the bridegroom. Kālidāsa gives graphic details of the performance of nuptials in accordance with the Vedic rites and local customs. The poet describes the joyful excitement of Umā's mother, Menā, on this occasion. She could place with great effort the auspicious painted mark on her daughter's forehead, and due to the dimness of her sight resulting from the tears of joy she inappropriately tied on Umā's arm the auspicious woollen thread which was later set right by her foster-mother. The eighth Canto contains a lascivious description of the amorous sports of the newly-wedded pair. Some critics censure Kālidāsa for such an obscene description of the conjugal ife of the divine pair.

The Raghuvaṃśa

The *Raghuvaṃśa* is Kālidāsa's another epic poem which is enumerated among the five famous *Mahākāvyas* of Sanskrit literature. It is regarded as the best specimen of a *Mahākāvya* according to the Sanskrit rhetoricians. Most of the modern scholars are of opinion that the *Raghuvaṃśa* was composed by Kālidāsa in his later age, as it refers to Yoga philosophy, employs grammatical similes, and reflects the maturity of his style and thought. It is worth noticing that several stanzas are common to both the epics (*supra*, Chapter I), and numerous verses in them exhibit similarity of ideas and expression. There is a striking difference between the *Kumārasambhava* and the *Raghuvaṃśa* in respect of descriptions and narratives. In the former the long descriptions of Nature and voluptuous beauty relegate the narative to the background, while the latter strikes, on the whole, a balance between the narratives and descriptions. However, Kālidāsa's poetic art in the *Raghuvaṃśa* is of no mean order, for this epic also affords us a wealth of telling similes, graphic descriptions, touching delineation of human sentiments, apt and suggestive expressions, wise sayings, and ideal characters. Although the *Raghuvaṃśa* amply illustrates Kālidāsa's maturity of thought and style, it cannot match the *Kumārasambhava* in the imaginative and fascinating description of Nature and youthful beauty. The *Raghuvaṃśa*, which is on the whole composed in a simple but effective style, has been characterized by some modern scholars as a gallery of brilliant pictures and as a string of several interesting episodes.

The theme of the epic *Raghuvaṃśa*, which literally means an account of Raghu's dynasty, is very vast indeed, covering as many as twenty kings of the Solar race. However, Kālidāsa's poetic genius has amply exploited this extensive theme to give full scope to his power of imagination in the description of varied scenes and situations such as the hermitage of Vasiṣṭha, Raghu's campaign of all-round conquest, battles, the *Svayaṃvara* and the wedding of Indumatī, Aja's heart-rending lamentation over the sudden death of Indumatī, the beauty of Spring, an aerial view of various sights of India during Rāma's return journey to Ayodhyā from Laṅkā in the aerial car, Sītā's pathetic condition after her abandonment in the forest and her highly spirited message to Rāma, and Kuśa's dream about the sad plight of Ayodhyā.

The *Raghuvaṃśa* contains nineteen Cantos at present. But some scholars opine that the epic originally had more Cantos and is incomplete in the present form, while others doubt the authenticity of the last two Cantos which appear to be inferior in poetic skill to the preceding ones. However, Mallinātha's commentary is available on these two Cantos also which seem to have been known to the author of the Aihole inscription, and which are quoted by some writers on poetics. So their authenticity is accepted by most of the modern scholars.

The poem opens with Kālidāsa's reverential obeisance to the universal parents, Pārvatī and Śiva. Expressing his humility and modesty, the poet compares his ambition of describing the great Solar race to an unwise attempt to cross the vast unfathomable ocean with the help of a raft, and observes that on account of his desire to win fame as a poet he would invite ridicule like a midget who greedily lifts up his arms to pluck a fruit that can be reached by a very tall person. However, he justifies his present work on the plea that in respect of the description of the Solar race already treated of by the earlier poets his own attempt is like a thread in a gem which has been already perforated with a hard instrument (or with a diamond). Kālidāsa begins the account of the Solar race with the ideal reign of King Dilīpa who was virtuous but had no issue. When the King accompanied by his queen Sudaksiṇā approached the sage Vasiṣṭha to seek his guidance and blessings, he was told by the sage that, as the King's negligence in showing reverence to the celestial cow Surabhi in the course of his visit to Indra infuriated her to inflict the curse of childlessness upon him, he should appease the celestial cow through the service of her daughter Nandinī at Vasiṣṭha's hermitage to obtain a son. By happy coincidence the cow Nandinī returned to the hermitage from the forest at that very moment when the sage was talking of her. Considering it to be a good augury, Vasiṣṭha advised the King and the Queen to tend the cow day and night. The King and the Queen accepted Vasiṣṭha's advice to appease the cow through service.

The second Canto contains a description of the King's faithful service to Nandinī and the test of his devotion to the cow. The Queen worshipped Nandinī in the hermitage every morning and evening, and the King followed the cow in the forest and did everything possible to make her happy and comfortable. Thus three weeks passed in the service of the cow. On the twenty-second day Nandinī entered a Himalayan cave to test the King's devotion, and was illusorily shown as attacked there by a lion. On hearing the cow's distressful bellowing, the King rushed to the cave, saw a lion sitting on the cow, and uplifted his right arm to pull out an arrow from the quiver to shoot down the lion. But the King's hand with its fingers touching the feathered part of an arrow stood still as if it were painted in a picture. Finding himself helpless due to the paralysis of his arm, the King burnt with rage like a snake whose power has been curbed by means of spells and herbs. Then the lion, addressing the King in human voice, told him that, as he (the lion) was Śiva's attendant appointed to guard Pārvatī's favourite pine tree (*Devadāru*) and allowed to subsist on animals straying there, the King should return without any feeling of shame, because he had already fully demonstrated his devotion to his preceptor; and that failure to protect that thing, which cannot be protected by means of a weapon, does not detract from the fame of a weapon-wielding hero. When the King offered his own body to the lion in exchange for Nandinī, the cow was pleased with the King and told him that it was just an illusion created by herself to test his devotion and that his desire for a son would be fulfilled. The King drank the milk of Nandinī to obtain a son as promised by the cow, and returned to his Capital with his wife who soon conceived Dilīpa's successor endowed with the great powers of the divine protectors of the world.

The third Canto is devoted to the description of the birth of Dilīpa's son Raghu, his childhood, education, youth, marriage, anointment as heir-apparent, heroic deeds in the discharge of his duty as a protector of the horse let loose by his father Dilīpa to perform the 100th horse-sacrifice, Raghu's brave fight against Indra who had stolen the sacrificial horse but later relented to award the fruit of the sacrifice without its final performance, and Raghu's assumption of kingship on the retirement of Dilīpa to the forest.

The fourth Canto contains a graphic account of Raghu's campaign of conquests in all directions. First of all he marched to the east with a formidable force, conquered all the eastern kings including those of *Suhma* and *Vaṅga* (Bengal), and erected pillars of victory on the islands between the streams of the Gaṅgā. Having crossed the river *Kapiśā* (*Kasai* in Midnapur District) on elephants, he advanced to the *Kaliṅga* country along the path shown by the people of the *Utkala* country, occupied the peak of the Mahendra mountain, defeated and captured the king of *Kaliṅga* who had opposed Raghu with elephants and arrows. But he (the king of Kaliṅga) was later released and made a vassal. Marching to the South along the eastern coast, Raghu crossed the river *Kāverī* and reached the foot of the *Malaya* mountain. The Pāṇḍya kings, who did not withstand Raghu's might, lay prostrate before him and paid him the tributes of their best pearls obtained from the ocean close to the mouth of the river *Tāmraparṇī.* Having enjoyed his stay at the *Malaya* and *Dardura* mountains abounding in sandal trees, Raghu crossed the *Sahya* mountain and conquered all kings on the western coast. Then he proceeded by the land route to conquer the Persian kings and defeated the western warriors equipped with a cavalry in a fierce fight. Consequently the battlefield was covered with their bearded heads looking like bee-hives. Then Raghu turned to the north and his horses relieved their fatigue by rolling on the banks of the river Oxus (*Vaṅkṣū* or *Vaṅkū* ; *see Note* 12 of Chapter II) and shook off the filaments of saffron sticking to their manes. After subduing the *Hūṇas* and the *Kambojas*, Raghu advanced towards the Himālayas, and conquered the hill tribes and the *Utsavasaṅketas.*[14] When Raghu crossed the river *Lauhityā* (*Brahmaputra*), the king of *Prāgjyotiṣa* trembling with fear did not withstand him and the lord of *Kāmarūpa* offered the tributes of elephants and gems to Raghu.[15] Thus concluding his victory in all quarters, Raghu triumphantly returned to his Capital and performed the *Viśvajit* sacrifice at which he gave away his entire wealth in charity.

The next four Cantos (V-VIII) are devoted to Raghu's son Aja. The fifth Canto narrates episodes concerning Aja's birth and his arrival in Kuṇḍinapura, the capital of Vidarbha, to attend Indumatī's *Svayaṃvara.* After Raghu's munificence had impoverished him, he was approached by a Snātaka named Kautsa, a pupil of Varatantu, for a donation of fourteen crores of golden coins to be presented to his (Kautsa's) preceptor as fees for receiving education. Expressing his inability to give the donation immediately, Raghu asked Kautsa to wait for a few days, and planned to storm Kubera's treasure for wealth. When Kubera came to know of Raghu's resolve, he (Kubera) voluntarily filled Raghu's treasury with wealth through a rain of gold coins. After taking the requisite amount of gold coins, Kautsa bestowed blessings on the King for the birth of a son. So Raghu was soon blessed with a son named Aja who resembled his father in appearance, valour and greatness. After Aja had acquired education and attained marriageable age, he was sent by his father Raghu to participate in the *Svayaṃvara* of Indumatī, the younger sister of the king of Vidarbha. On his way when Aja encamped his fatigued force on the bank of the river Narmadā, his camp was suddenly attacked by a wild elephant which, on being hit by Aja's arrow in the forehead, turned into a Gandharva condemned by a curse, and which gratefully presented Aja with a magic weapon called *Sammohana* that could put an enemy force to sleep. On his arrival at Kuṇḍinapura, the capital of Vidarbha, Aja was cordially received by the king of Vidarbha and lodged in a beautiful new palace. There Aja slept late and passed the night, eagerly looking forward to the result of the *Svayaṃvara.*

The sixth Canto contains a vivid description of the *Svayaṃvara.* On arrival in the *Svayaṃvara-hall* Aja saw kings seated on high couches, and he took his seat in their midst. As soon as Indumatī escorted by her companion Sunandā entered the assembly-hall, all the suitors turned their attention to her (Indumatī). The Princess passed by the kings one by one, while her companion Sunandā introduced each one of them detailing his genealogy and distinguishing features. Kālidāsa describes the condition of the rejected kings by the following simile of a moving lamp-flame (*dīpa-śikhā*): "As soon as Indumatī passed by a king (rejecting him), he became crest-fallen and colourless like a highway turret which has been left behind by a moving lamp-flame at night." This simile has earned the poet the epithet of *Dīpaśikhā-Kālidāsa.* When Indumatī reached Aja, she fell in love with him at first sight and asked her companion to put the bridal garland around his neck.

The seventh Canto describes their wedding and subsequent journey to Ayodhyā. The wedding rites are performed with great pomp and show. The ladies of the Capital are portrayed as rushing to the windows of their houses in haste to have a glimpse of the couple (*supra,* Chapter II). After the wedding when Aja was returning to Ayodhyā with Indumatī, he was attacked by the rejected kings to wreak vengeance upon him and to snatch away Indumatī. Aja defeated them with the help of his above-mentioned magic weapon gifted to him by the Gandharva, and returned victoriously to his father Raghu who decided to retire to the forest after handing over the kingdom to him.

The eighth Canto contains a description of Aja's efficient and popular administration and his pathetic lamentation over the sudden death of his dear wife Indumatī. Aja, who ruled righteously, was as popular among his subjects as Raghu. A son named Daśaratha was born to Aja. When Raghu died after subduing his senses as a hermit, all the honours due to a Yogin's funeral were accorded to him. One day while Aja was sporting with Indumatī in a garden, Nārada was passing that way through the sky and a garland of celestial flowers placed on his lute was blown by a strong wind to the breast of Indumatī who immediately fell down and expired on the mere touch of the garland. Then Aja also collapsed and became unconscious. After regaining consciousness he took her body in his lap and lamented so pathetically that his poignant pathos moved even trees to tears of sorrowful sympathy. After her cremation Aja passed his time in extreme sorrow and grief. Vasiṣṭha's sagacious message of consolation, disclosing Indumatī's real identity as an Apsaras released by the fall of the garland from her curse of mortal bondage, had no effect on the King who could not forget his beloved. He remained griefstricken and disconsolate for eight long years after which he handed over the kingdom to his son Daśaratha and left his mortal frame at the confluence of the rivers Gaṅgā and Sarayū to seek permanent union with his beloved in heaven.

The ninth Canto is devoted to a brilliant description of Daśaratha's able administration, his three marriages, performance of sacrifices, the Spring season, and his hunting-excursion in the forest. In the course of his hunting-excursion Daśaratha one day early in the morning heard on the bank of the river Tamasā the sound of filling a pitcher with water, mistook it for the trumpet of an elephant, and shot an arrow aiming at the sound. When the King heard a piteous human cry "O Father", he rushed there and found an ascetic's son pierced with the arrow. Daśaratha took the wounded boy to his aged parents who were so much griefstricken at their only son's death that they requested the King to prepare a funeral pyre for them along with that of their son. Before entering the funeral pyre the old ascetic cursed Daśaratha that he, too, would die of the grief of his son's separation in old age. Daśaratha took this curse as a mixed blessing in the sense that he who was then without a son would have at least one.

The next six Cantos (X-XV) are devoted to Rāma. The tenth Canto describes the birth of Daśaratha's four sons, namely, Rāma, Lakṣmaṇa, Bharata and Śatrughna, following the performance of a sacrifice for the purpose. Rāma is portrayed as an incarnation of Viṣṇu to punish Rāvaṇa for his misdeeds. The eleventh Canto contains an account of the help rendered by the young princes, Rāma and Lakṣmaṇa, to the Sage Viśvāmitra in the performance of his sacrifices which were disturbed by the demons; of Rāma's marriage with Sītā at Mithilā after his victory in the *Svayaṃvara*, and of Paraśurāma's discomfiture at the hands of Rāma. In Canto XII Kālidāsa displays his descriptive power in vividly narrating the well-known events of Rāma's life, viz., his exile, sojourn at Pañchavaṭī, Sītā's abduction by Rāvaṇa, Rāma's alliance with Sugrīva, Vālin's death, Hanumat's crossing the ocean and locating Sītā in Laṅkā, Rāma's march to Laṅkā with an army of monkeys, the famous battle between Rāma and Rāvaṇa, Rāvaṇa's death at the hands of Rāma, Sīta's fire-ordeal, and the departure of Rāma, Sītā and Lakṣmaṇa to Ayodhyā by an aerial car called *Puṣpaka*. The thirteenth Canto contains an imaginative and fascinating description of the various aspects of Indian landscape as viewed by Rāma from the aerial car. Then follows a description of the warm reception accorded to Rāma and his companions by Bharata and the citizens of Ayodhyā. The fourteenth Canto opens with the portrayal of a happy picture of Rāma and Sītā in Ayodhyā but ends with the touching description of Sītā's pathetic plight in abandonment. On their arrival in Ayodhyā Rāma and Sītā visited the widows of King Daśaratha to greet them. After Rāma had been crowned King, he began to rule righteously and to lead a happy conjugal life in the company of his beloved wife Sītā. However, their happiness proved to be short-lived, as some citizens of Ayodhyā began to talk scandalously about Sītā's stay in Laṅkā. Although Rāma was fully convinced of the purity of Sītā, he had to swallow the bitter pill of abandoning his pregnant wife in order to discharge his harsh duty as an ideal King. At Rāma's behest Lakṣmaṇa escorted Sītā in a chariot to a desolate place near Vālmīki's hermitage on the bank of the river Gaṅgā. Sītā accompanied him happily without suspecting any thing untoward, as she had once expressed her desire to Rāma to revisit the penance-groves on the bank of the Gaṅgā. When Lakṣmaṇa disclosed to Sītā the real purpose of his mission, she fell into a swoon. On regaining consciousness she did not utter a word of reproach against Rāma and requested Lakṣmaṇa to convey her message to King Rāma:[15] "Is it in keeping with the reputation of your family that you should repudiate me whose purity was tested in the fire?" After Lakṣmaṇa's departure she cried so pathetically that the entire forest presented a picture of sorrowful grief in sympathy with her. The peacocks ceased their dance, the trees shed flowers, and the female deer did not eat the blades of grass held in their mouths. On hearing Sītā's message Rāma burst into tears, but restrained himself and carried out his duties of administration with a he vy heart. He never thought of another woman and took Sītā's statue as his partner in the performance of the Aśvamedha sacrifice. Vālmīki gave shelter to Sītā in his hermitage and looked after her.

The fifteenth Canto covers the remaining story of Rāma's life up to his ascent to heaven. Rāma's brother Śatrughna killed the demon Lavaṇa at Rāma's behest and founded the city of *Mathurā* on the bank of the river Yamunā, Sītā gave birth to twin sons who were named Lava and Kuśa, and who were brought up and educated by Vālmīki. He made them recite his *Rāmāyaṇa.* The twin brothers consoled Sītā and delighted people by reciting the deeds of Rāma. During the performance of the Aśvamedha sacrifice when Rāma was staying in a sacrificial hut with Sītā's golden statue as her representative, he along with his brothers heard the recital of the *Rāmāyaṇa* by Kuśa and Lava and recognized them as his sons. Rāma then approached Vālmīki who asked him to take back Sītā. Rāma said that though Sītā was pure, she should convince his people about her purity. Sītā appeared before Rāma, swore her purity by water, and prayed to her mother Earth to take her back in her bosom if she was pure. As soon as she uttered these words, a halo of light suddenly flashed from an opening of the earth and the Goddess Earth appeared there seated on a throne. After taking Sītā in her lap, the Goddess at once disappeared into the earth, disregarding Rāma's entreaty not to snatch away Sītā. Having handed over the kingdom of Kuśāvatī to Kuśa and that of Śarāvatī to Lava, Rāma, accompanied by his brothers and citizens, went out of Ayodhyā to the river Sarayū. From there he proceeded to heaven in a celestial chariot, after making this river as a staircase to heaven for his followers.

Cantos XVI-XIX are devoted to the descendants of Rāma. The sixteenth Canto contains an account of the desolation and rehabilitation of Ayodhyā. Kuśa, while reigning from his capital city of Kuśāvatī, once saw at dead of night a strange woman dressed like a lady whose husband is abroad. On Kuśa's enquiries she disclosed her identity as the presiding deity of the city of Ayodhyā, described the deplorable condition of the desolate city, and requested him to rehabilitate it by shifting his capital there. In response to her request Kuśa shifted his capital to Ayodhyā which then regained her lost glory. This Canto ends with the story of Kuśa's marriage with Kumudvatī, the younger sister of the Nāga king Kumuda.

Cantos XVII-XIX, which lack both in interest and poetic excellence characteristically associated with Kālidāsa, seem to be no more than a rough draft as aptly observed by Keith.[17] Although some scholars[18] doubt the authenticity of these Cantos, they are commented upon by Mallinātha and several other commentators and seem to be known to the author of the Aihole inscription.[19]

In Canto XVII, which describes the efficient and admirable administration of Kuśa's son Atithi born of Kumudvatī, the poet attempts to show off his knowledge of statecraft. Canto XVIII is little more than a catalogue of the names of about two dozen descendants of the Solar dynasty following Atithi. The epic abruptly ends with Canto XIX in which the poet displays his knowledge of erotics by way of describing the debauchery of Raghu's degenerate descendant, King Agnivarṇa, who met with a premature death due to consumption caused by his excessive indulgence in sensual pleasures. His enceinte Queen, who was made Regent by his ministers and subjects, properly administered the kingdom with the assistance of noble and elderly ministers for the welfare of the people who were waiting for the birth of his successor.

Notes and References

1. Cf. Ragh. XV, 41.
2. R. IV, 19, 28; VI, 113, 26, etc.; cf. Vik., p. 9.
3. *See*, *India of Vedic Kalpasūtras*, pp. 104ff, for the division of a year into six seasons.
4. RS. III, 2.
5. Cf., e.g., R. IV, 28, 24-RS. II, 5.
6. The number of stanzas in the *Meghadūta* varies from 110 to 120 according to the commentators of the text.
7. *Rāmagiri* is identified by V.V. Mirashi (*Kalidāsa*, 1969, pp. 152-53) and B.S. Upadhyaya (*India in Kālidāsa*, 1968, p. 19) with the *Ramtek* hill lying at a distance of about 28 miles from Nagpur. There is a lake at the foot of this hill with beautiful natural scenery. But some scholars doubt this identification and identify *Rāmagiri* with other hills, such as *Rāmgaḍh*, a hill in Orissa, or a hill situated in *Daṇḍakāraṇya*.
8. Some scholars explain *Vananadī* or *Naganadī* (the first member of the compound) as the name of a particular river, whereas others take it as a common noun in the plural signifying "forest rills".
9. The river *Sindhu* (Pūrvamegha, 29) is probably the modern *Kāli Sindh*, a tributary of the Chambal; and the *Nirvindhyā* may be identified with the modern *Newuj*, another tributary of the Chambal between the Betwa and the Kālī Sindh; cf. B.S. Upadhyaya, *op. cit.*, pp. 18-19. B.C. Law's identification (*Geographical Aspects of Kālidāsa's Works*, Calcutta, 1954, p. 32) of this *Sindhu* with the river Indus is patently erroneous; see also pp. 37-38. Mallinātha explains the word *Sindhu* here as a river referring to the *Nirvindhyā* mentioned in the preceding stanza.
10. *See* Note 8 of Chapter I.
11. सीतां प्रति रामस्य हनुमत्संदेशं मनसि
    निधाय मेघसंदेशं कविः कृतवानित्याहुः ।
    (Mallinātha on verse 1 of the Megh.)
12. The Rāmāyaṇa (I, 35-37) describes Himālaya and Menā as the parents of Umā, her austerities to attain Śiva, their marriage, and the birth of Kumāra. In a Brāhmaṇa-like prose passage the Mbh. (XII, 342,62) narrates the story that Rudra as well as Bhṛgu desired to marry Himālaya's daughter Umā, and that Bhṛgu cursed Himālaya who had

rejected Bhṛgu's request for Umā's hand. It shows that the legend of Umā's marriage with Śiva was already current in the Epic times in different versions. The version of this legend contained in the *Pārvati-khaṇḍa* of the *Mahāśiva-Purāṇa* is obviously an imitation of the KS.

13. KS. VII, 56-66-Ragh. VII, 5-14; KS. VII, 73-Ragh. VII, 19.
14. The *Utsava-saṅketas* are identified by some scholars with the people of Ladakh; *cf.*, Mirashi, *op. cit.*, p. 167. According to the Mbh. (II, 27, 16), Arjuna in the course of his *Dig-vijaya* defeated seven *Utsavasaṅketa* tribes before conquering Kashmir. It shows that the *Utsavasaṅketas* were some hill tribes inhabiting the region adjoining Kashmir. Mallinātha also explains the *Utsavasaṅketas* as tribes (*gaṇas*).
15. Since *Prāgjyotiṣa* and *Kāmarūpa* are regarded as synonymous by several later writers, Mark Collins (*Geographical Data of the Raghuvaṃśa and Daśakumāracharita*, Leipzig, 1907, p. 15) opines that the mention of *Prāgjyotiṣa* and *Kāmarūpa* as two distinct kingdoms in the Ragh. betrays Kālidāsa's fallacy. B. S. Upadhyāya (*India in Kalidasa*, Delhi, 1968, p. 63) controverts the above-referred opinion of Mark Collins and puts forward the view that Kālidāsa does not treat the two as different kingdoms but refers to the single kingdom of *Kāmarūpa* with its capital at *Prāgjyotiṣa*, modern Gauhati. Although Mallinātha seems to explain *Prāgjyotiṣa* and *Kāmarūpa* as two separate kingdoms and some later texts, such as the *Kālikā-Purāṇa* (Chapter 38) mention *Prāgjyotiṣa* as the capital of *Kāmarūpa*, Kālidāsa appears to use these two terms as synonyms. He first employs the term *Prāgjyotiṣa* and later on its synonym *Kāmarūpa* to avoid repetition, just as Bāṇa in his *Harṣacharita* (pp. 214, 220, 221, 225) employs both *Prāgjyotiṣa* and *Kāmarūpa* to denote one and the same kingdom.
16. Ragh. VI, 67 (see Note 20 of Chapter V).
17. Keith, *A History of Sanskrit Literature*, p. 97.
18. *Cf.* Hillebrandt, *Kālidāsa*, pp. 42ff.
19. Keith, *op. cit.*, p. 97, f.n. 1.

4

The Dramatic Art of Kālidāsa

Kālidāsa ranks among the foremost dramatists of the world and is styled as the Shakespeare of India by some modern scholars. There is a rare combination of poetic imagination and dramatic genius in Kālidāsa. He is unsurpassed in richness of creative fancy, delineation of tender emotions, elegance and felicity of expression, harmony of sound and sense, and sharpness of characterisation.

There is no doubt that he was preceded by such renowned playwrights as *Bhāsa, Saumilla* and *Kaviputra* mentioned in the prologue of the *Mālavikāgnimitra*. However, Kālidāsa's towering fame as a dramatist *par excellence* pushed the plays of his predecessors into oblivion, although thirteen anonymous plays discovered by T. Ganapati Sastri of Trivandrum in 1912 are now ascribed by most of the modern scholars to Bhāsa in view of certain characteristic features of these plays, while a few scholars doubt their authenticity. We may briefly point out that the development of *dramatic art* coupled with style, metres and the Prākrits employed in the dramas ascribed to Bhāsa betokens their priority to Kālidāsa's plays. Moreover, the dramas ascribed to Bhāsa do not betray the influence of Kālidāsa and conform to the characteristics of Bhāsa's plays mentioned by Bāṇa in his *Harṣacharita*. Therefore, it would not be unreasonable to accept the authenticity of the Trivandrum dramas ascribed to Bhāsa. Although some scholars see Bhāsa's influence on Kālidāsa in respect of ideas and expressions, the evidence is too tenuous to merit serious consideration. We should not overlook the obvious fact that Kālidāsa never imitates but creates new word-pictures, conceives original ideas, and coins felicitous expressions. As regards the fragments of Sanskrit dramas ascribed to Aśvaghoṣa, we have already discussed above in Chapter II the relative chronology of Kālidāsa and Aśvaghoṣa. Moreover, Aśvaghoṣa's name as a Sanskrit dramatist does not figure in any important work of antiquity. Therefore, it would be gratuitous to assume that the fragmentary dramas ascribed to Aśvaghoṣa are anterior to the plays of Kālidāsa. Similarly the date of the *Mṛchchhakaṭika* ascribed to King *Śūdraka* is highly doubtful, and it cannot be regarded with certainty as a precursor of Kālidāsa's plays.

Some modern scholars see a gradual development in Kālidāsa's dramatic art from the *Mālavikāgnimitra* and the *Vikramorvaśīya* to the *Śākuntala.* In fact the Śakuntala exhibits the perfection of Kālidāsa's art in its various aspects—ingenuity of the plot, flight of imagination, unique delineation of human feelings and characters, elegance and simplicity of expression, fusion of sound and sense, sympathetic description of Nature, and a wonderful blend of natural and supernatural elements. That the Śākuntala shows a definite development not only in Kālidāsa's dramatic art but also in his poetic art is clearly demonstrated by the improvement effected by him in this drama[1] upon the delineation of the theme of Nature's sympathy with human feelings previously attempted by him in his Ragh.[2] In the drama the creepers are depicted as shedding tears in the form of pale leaves to express their sorrow at Śakuntalā's departure, whereas the Ragh. describes the trees as shedding flowers in sympathy with abandoned Sītā. The rest of the theme—the peacocks ceasing their dance and the female deer dropping grass-morsels from their mouths—is common to both the works. It is obvious that the metaphorical description of creepers shedding tears in the form of pale leaves is much more apt and expressive than the one which describes the flowers of trees as their tears.

Although the Māl. and the Vik. do not show the maturity and perfection of Kālidāsa's dramatic art attained in the Śak., yet these two earlier dramas also reveal his dramatic genius in no small measure. He displays his originality in the construction of their plots, in the invention of new situations and incidents, in effective characterisation, in the delineation of sentiments, and in the choice of ideas and expressions. Kālidāsa's dramatic genius exhibited in the *Mālavikāgnimitra* influenced several later playwrights like Śrīharṣa and Rājaśekhara to model the plot of their dramas on the Māl.

Love is the common theme of all the three plays composed by Kālidāsa, but his approach in each play is fresh and original. The Māl. depicts the love-affair between a middle-aged married king and a princess living incognito in his harem as a handmaid of his chief queen, culminating in their marriage after many obstacles, while the Vik. is a drama of love between a celestial nymph and a mortal king with scenes full of poignant pathos at their separation on account of the intervention of supernatural powers. Love in the Śak. is elevated by Kālidāsa from earth to heaven and is purified like gold in the fire of separation and repentence. In the Māl., which is the work of his youthful days, Kālidāsa is eagar to show off his knowledge of the technicalities of dance and dramaturgy, but he does not pay adequate attention to the delineation of Nature in this play as in his other two plays. His all the three plays contain a large number of verses exhibiting his poetic art side by side with his dramatic genius. For instance, the Śak. contains nearly two hundred stanzas. In view of such a large number of verses these dramas are described by some modern critics as dramatic poems. However, this criticism is not justified, for the plays can be successfully staged by competent actors and actresses. These plays were written for such audience as could enjoy their dramatic beauty as much as their poetic excellence. Therefore, only those critics who think that the stanzas impede dramatic action find fault in Kālidāsa's plays. It would be more appropriate to describe them as poetic plays, because poetry heightens their dramatic effect. The audience in ancient India did not appreciate purely prosaic plays.

We shall now briefly discuss the chief characteristics of each of the three plays.

The Mālavikāgnimitra

The *Mālavikāgnimitra* depicts in five Acts the love-affair between the Śuṅga king Agnimitra of Vidiśā and the Vidarbha princess Mālavikā who was residing in his harem incognito as a maid-servant of his chief Queen Dhāriṇī due to untoward circumstances. This historical story has been skilfully interwoven by Kālidāsa into a complicated plot. There seems to be no basis for the view advanced by some scholars that Kālidāsa composed the play to honour his patron King Agnimitra, because it seems to be inconceivable that Kālidāsa could have made his patron King prostrate at the feet of his junior Queen and could have painted his character in such an unfavourable light in comparison with the ideal personalities of the Ragh. The contrary view is that the play is a veiled satire on some royal family of Kālidāsa's time, if not on Agnimitra himself.[3] The most plausible explanation appears to be that the love-story of Mālavikā and Agnimitra might have been current in Kālidāsa's time as part of popular folklore, like the story of Udayana and Vāsavadattā; and that the dramatic genius of our playwright turned it into a full-fledged play. So there seems to be no valid reason for reading any political, social or personal motive into the play.

In Act I the Prologue is followed by an Interlude in which two maid-servants, Bakulāvalikā and Kaumudikā, deputed by the chief Queen Dhāriṇī, converse at their chance-meeting about the purpose of their respective visits. The former says that she is going to the dance master Gaṇadāsa to enquire about the progress made by Mālavikā in dancing, and the latter tells the former that she (Kaumudikā) is carrying to the Queen from a goldsmith a signet ring with the figure of a snake engraved on it. It is further revealed in their conversation that when the King happened to see Mālavikā's portrait in a group painting of Queen Dhāriṇī with her servants, he enquired from the Queen about the identity of that portrait, and on the Queen's hesitation to disclose her identity the child princess Vasumatī blurted out that she was Mālavikā. Bakulāvalikā informs that since then the Queen is taking every possible care to keep Mālavikā out of the King's sight. On Bakulāvalikā's enquiry about the progress made by Mālavikā in dancing, the dance master Gaṇadāsa praises Mālavikā's talent in dancing and enquires about her family and antecedents from Bakulāvalikā who tells him that Mālavikā was sent as a present to the Queen by her step-brother Vīrasena who is the commander in charge of the King's frontier-fortress on the banks of the river Narmadā.

In the scene following the Interlude King Agnimitra is shown as holding consultation with his minister. It is revealed in their conversation that in a political upheaval in Vidarbha Yajñasena, a relative of the prime minister of the ousted Maurya King, usurped the throne of that country and detained his cousin Mādhavasena, the rightful heir to the throne, while the latter was attempting to flee to Vidiśā to seek Agnimitra's help and to offer him the hand of his (Mādhavasena's) sister. The King Agnimitra in his communication to Yajñasena had demanded the release of Mādhavasena alongwith his family, but Yajñasena refused to do so and informed Agnimitra that Mādhavasena's sister was lost in the turmoil following his detention. Then Agnimitra orders military operations against Yajñasena.

After the minister's exit the Jester (*Vidūṣaka*) enters the stage and informs the King that a stratagem has been contrived by which the King wo ld be able to see Mālavikā. Just then the voices of two contestants for superiority in dance are heard behind the curtain. The two dance masters, Queen Dhāriṇī's protégé Gaṇadāsa and the King's protégé Haradatta, enter the stage and request the King to adjudge their relative merits in the art of dancing. But the King refuses to act as a judge and proposes that their contest should be held in the presence of the Queen also. In accordance with this proposal the Queen is invited there together with the nun Kauśikī. After their arrival it is decided that each of the two contestants would be judged on the basis of the performance of his pupil in dancing, and that the nun Kauśikī would act as a judge. The Queen sees through the game, but she is helpless. On hearing the sound of a drum announcing the completion of arrangements for a contest in dancing, all leave for the theatre.

Act II opens with a brief dialogue between the King and the nun about the priority to be accorded in the contest. It is decided by the nun that Gaṇadāsa should first take the test of his ability by presenting the dance performance of his pupil Mālavikā. Accordingly Mālavikā appears on the stage, sings a song of love, and displays her skill to demonstrate the different moods in the song by gestures of dance. Her performance is adjudged as excellent and flawless. The King who is extremely delighted to see her ravishing beauty is enamoured of her. At the time of her departure a witty remark made by the Jester makes her smile, and the King again beholds her in a cheerful mood and feels fascinated by her voluptuous beauty. It is declared that the performance of Haradatta's pupil would be tested on the following day, as the King is getting late for his bath and meals.

In the beginning of Act III there is an Interlude in which it is revealed through a dialogue between Kauśikī's female attendant Samāhitikā and the female-guard of the royal pleasure-garden Madhukarikā that though the King is deeply in love with Mālavikā yet he refrains from doing anything to express it openly for fear of hurting the feelings of his Queen Dhāriṇī; that Mālavikā is languishing in her love for the King; and that even after the advent of Spring the Queen's favourite golden Aśoka tree has not yet blossomed, as its desire for being kicked by a lovely maiden with her decorated foot has not been fulfilled.

The scene following the Interlude shows the love-sick King in a depressed mood in the company of the Jester who tries to cheer him up with the assurance of arranging a secret meeting between him and Mālavikā. The Jester reminds the King to keep his promise of giving company to his younger Queen Irāvatī at a swing-festival in the pleasure-garden. After some hesitation the King agrees to fulfil his promise, and both of them go to the pleasure-garden where the Jester catches sight of Mālavikā instead of Irāvatī and informs the King. Then the King and the Jester hide behind a thicket of creepers, watch Mālavikā's movements and overhear her words. She goes to the golden Aśoka tree and loudly talks to herself of her deep love for the King who feels elated on hearing her confession of love. In the meantime Bakulāvalikā arrives there, decorates Mālavikā's feet with red dye, and talks to her about her love. The younger Queen Irāvatī also arrives there with her attendant Nipuṇikā, and secretly overhears the conversation of Mālavikā and Bakulāvalikā, on the one hand, and that of the King and the Jester on the other. As soon as Mālavikā kicks the golden Aśoka tree with her foot, the King along with the Jester appears before her and requests her to satisfy his longing. On hearing his words, enraged Irāvatī rushes out of her hiding and rebukes both the King and Mālavikā. The King begs Irāvatī's forgiveness, but she is in no mood to relent and stops short of hitting him with her girdle. He then lies prostrate at her feet to conciliate her, but she leaves the place in anger.

Act IV opens with the love-sick King bemoaning his frustration in love. He sends his door-keeper to Queen Dhāriṇī to enquire about her sprained ankle, and asks the Jester about Mālavikā. The Jester tells him that on Irāvatī's complaint Queen Dhāriṇī has detained both Mālavikā and Bakulāvalikā in an underground cellar and ordered the guard not to release them without seeing her (Queen's) signet ring as token of her authority. The Jester devises a stratagem for their release. The King goes to Queen Dhāriṇī who is confined to bed on account of her sprained ankle and who is hearing a story from Kauśikī. After a short while the Jester also enters there crying that he has been bitten by a snake in the act of plucking flowers for the Queen. He is sent for treatment to a physician who conveys the request that, unless something with the figure of a snake engraved upon it is made available for immersion in water, his treatment will not be effective. The Queen offers her own signet ring for the purpose. However, the Jester secures the release of Mālavikā and Bakulāvalikā by showing the ring to the guard of the underground cellar on the false plea that the King has ordered the release of all prisoners in compliance with the advice of astrologers to ward off the evil effect of an unfavourable constellation. The message of the Jester's cure is conveyed to the Queen, and a request from the minister is sent to the King to attend to an important official work. Under this pretext the King takes leave of Queen Dhāriṇī and goes straight to the pleasure-garden where the Jester tells him about Mālavikā's release and leads him to the summer-house to meet his beloved. After Bakulāvalikā and the Jester have been sent away, both the lovers lovingly talk to each other to their hearts' content in complete privacy. The Jester, who falls asleep on the terrace of the summer-house, is sighted by Queen Irāvatī who accompanied by her attendant Nipuṇikā comes there. She (Irāvatī) sees the King with Mālavikā and upbraids him. At that very moment the King receives the message that his daughter Vasulakṣmī frightened by a monkey is lying unconscious in the lap of her mother (Dhāriṇī). Irāvatī and the King rush there, and thus he is saved from an embarrassing situation. Mālavikā also heaves a sigh of relief and is pleased to learn that the golden Aśoka tree kicked by her has blossomed, as Queen Dhāriṇī had promised to grant her a wish on the blossoming of this tree.

In the beginning of Act V there is an Interlude in which the female garden-keeper Madhukarikā and the hunch-back Sārasika, a servant of Queen Dhāriṇī, reveal through their conversation that the chief Queen has been daily offering gold coins in charity to ensure the safety of her son Vasumitra who has been appointed by his grandfather Puṣyamitra to guard the sacrificial horse; and that Agnimitra's commander Vīrasena has routed the Vidarbha King Yajñasena and released Mādhavasena who has sent an ambassador with a large amount of precious gems, vehicles, and a number of maids well-versed in arts as gifts to King Agnimitra.

In the scene following the Interlude Queen Dhāriṇī makes preparation for the celebrations of blossoming of the golden Aśoka tree, and conveys her request to the King to grace the function with his presence. The King and the Jester go to the pleasure-garden, and the former is delighted to find Mālavikā attired in nuptial dress and decked with ornaments. At that time two female dancers, sent as presents by Mādhavasena and ushered in before Agnimitra by the chamberlain, recognize Mālavikā as the younger sister of Mādhavasena, and Kauśikī as the widowed sister of his minister Sumati who laid down his own life to save Mālavikā from the clutches of robbers on her way to Vidiśā. Then Kauśikī discloses that, though she was also wounded in the robbers' attack and came to Vidiśā on regaining consciousness, she refrained from revealing Mālavikā's identity because she (Kauśikī) knew of a prophecy according to which Mālavikā is to marry a worthy husband after passing one year as a servant. In the meantime, Puṣyamitra sends the happy tidings that Agnimitra's son Vasumitra has defeated the Yavanas on the bank of the Indus;

and he (Puṣyamitra) invites Agnimitra alongwith his Queen to attend the performance of the horse-sacrifice. The kingdom of Vidarbha is equally divided by King Agnimitra between Mādhavasena and Yajñasena with the river *Varadā* (*Wārdhā*) serving as the boundary line. Queen Dhāriṇī, who is overjoyed at the happy news of his son's victory, puts a veil on Mālavikā and presents her to the King who gladly accepts her after feigning abashment. Thus the play ends on a happy note.

Kālidāsa's power of characterization is amply exhibited in the Māl. Mālavikā, the heroine of the play, is portrayed as a very beautiful, charming, intelligent, modest, cultured, considerate, sincere, and youthful maiden. The King tells the Vidūṣaka that, on seeing her portrait in the painting, he (King) previously doubted whether she was really as beautiful as painted in the picture, but now when he sees her in person he finds her more beautiful than her picture. The King describes her ravishing beauty as follows :[1]

"Her face with large eyes looks beautiful like the autumnal moon. Her lovely arms are bent at the shoulders. Her bosom is compact with buxom and prominent breasts. Her sides are so shapely, as if they have been chiselled. Her waist is so slender that it can be grasped with a single hand, while her beautiful buttocks are large. The toes of her feet are beautifully curved. In short, her charming form conforms to the ideal of a dancing beauty conceived by the dance master." Mālavikā is so intelligent that she learns dance very quickly and displays her extraordinary skill in dance before the audience. She is constant in her love and courageously endures all sufferings for the sake of her love.

Kālidāsa depicts the characters of Dhāriṇī and Irāvatī in contrasting colours. The chief Queen Dhāriṇī is elderly, sober, patient, graceful and magnanimous, and commands the respect of all. Although she does everything possible in her power to keep Mālavikā out of the King's sight, yet when she (Dhāriṇī) realises that the King's love-affair has reached the point of no return she herself offers the hand of Mālavikā to him. As an affectionate mother she prays and offers charities for the safety and victory of his son Vasumitra. She is kindly disposed towards her servants.

On the contrary, Irāvatī who is young, impulsive, irascible and impetuous betrays her jealousy towards Mālavikā, and puts obstacles in the King's love-affair. Irāvatī keeps an eye on the King's amorous manoeuvres, appears on the scene twice to thwart his plan to be close to Mālavikā, upbraids him, and once raises her girdle to strike him, but stops short of hitting him. Unlike Dhāriṇī, Irāvatī is not prepared to reconcile herself to the King's marriage with Mālavikā, and therefore absents herself from the scene of final union between the King and Mālavikā, though she (Irāvatī) sends a formal message of congratulations.

The nun Kauśikī is portrayed as a learned and saintly lady who speaks Sanskrit. Due to her widowhood and the ghastly assassination of her brother Sumati at the hands of robbers she renounced the world and became a nun, but she did not give up her interest in the affairs of the world. She is favourably disposed towards Mālavikā and lends her support to the Vidūṣaka's stratagems to bring about union between the King and Mālavikā. Kauśikī is adept in dance and story-telling. Therefore, she acts as a judge in the dancing contest and entertains Queen Dhāriṇī with stories. The nun is highly respected by the King who compares her to spiritual knowledge.

Kālidāsa depicts the hero of the play, King Agnimitra, as brave, shrewd and gallant. He shows his political wisdom by first warning the Vidarbha king Yajñasena to release his rival cousin Mādhavasena and then by dividing the kingdom of Vidarbha between Mādhavasena and Yajñasena after Yajñasena's defeat at the hands of Vīrasena. However, Agnimitra's love-affair with a maid-servant of his chief Queen does not paint his character in a favourable light at least in the eyes of modern critics. Although the King is a middle-aged man with two wives and a grown-up son, yet Agnimitra pines for a young maid-servant and contrives stratagems in league with the Jester to secure union with her. A bright aspect of his character is that he shows due regard to the feelings of his two Queens, even lies prostrate at the feet of her younger Queen Irāvatī to beg her forgiveness for his love-affair with Mālavikā, and never exercises his imperial authority to fulfil his desire for union with Mālavikā.

The role of the Vidūṣaka, Gautama, as a real jester is insignificant, and he is portrayed mainly as the King's confidant, counsellor and companion in his love-intrigues.

The Vikramorvaśīya

The Five-Act play *Vikramorvaśīya*, which literally means "a play in which *Urvaśī* is won by valour (*Vikrama*)", is available in two different recensions—the Northern recension and the Southern recension. In the Northern recension the play is styled as a *Troṭaka* and contains in Act IV a number of Apabhraṃśa verses with directions about their mode of singing, whereas the Southern recension omits these verses and calls the play a *Nāṭaka*. Most of the modern scholars doubt the authenticity of the Apabhraṃśa verses contained in the Northern recension on the grounds that there is some discrepancy between these verses and the prose of the play, and that the type of Apabhraṃśa found in these verses does not appear to be of such an early date as the dramas of Kālidāsa.

Kālidāsa has skilfully constructed the plot of the play with the elements of an ancient mythological legend relating to the love-affair of a mortal king Purūravas and a celestial nymph Urvaśī. In addition to the Ṛgvedic Hymn (X, 95) containing the dialogue between Urvaśī and Purūravas, various versions of the legend are found in the later works such as the *Śatapatha Brāhmaṇa*, the *Baudhāyana Śrautasūtra*, the *Bṛhaddevatā*, the *Sarvānukramaṇī*, the *Kathāsaritsāgara* and several *Purāṇas*, viz., the *Matsya-Purāṇa*, the *Viṣṇu-Purāṇa*, the *Padma-Purāṇa*, the *Bhāgavata-Purāṇa*, the *Vāyu-Purāṇa*, the *Brahmāṇḍa-Purāṇa*, the *Viṣṇudharmottara-Purāṇa*, the *Devībhāgavata-Purāṇa* and the *Harivaṃśa*. A critical and comparative study of the different versions of the legend has been made by many eminent scholars including K. F. Geldner.[5]

It is important to note that Kālidāsa does not follow blindly any of the earlier versions of the legend. He has adapted some essential features of the ancient legend to construct the plot of the play in which he has ingeniously introduced a number of new incidents and situations to heighten its dramatic effect. Kālidāsa seems to have purposely chosen this legend with a view to dramatizing the close relationship between mortals and heavenly beings.

The Vik., which shares some important features with the Śak., appears to be its precursor. The plots of both the plays are based on mythological legends. The heroine of the Vik. is a nymph, and that of the Śak. is the daughter of a nymph. The heroes and heroines in both the plays fall in love at first sight. The scenes in both the plays shift from earth to heaven and vice versa. In both the dramas the lovers are separated by a curse, but they are later reunited by means of a magic device which consists of a jewel in the Vik., and of a ring in the Śak. In both the plays the heroes are unconsciously attracted by the unknown paternal affection towards their sons at their first chance-meeting, and similarly they express delight at the first sight of their sons.[6] In the Vik. Āyus is shown as playing with a peacock, while Bharata in the Śak. sports with a lion cub. In the Vik. the heroine Urvaśī turns back to see her lover Purūravas on the pretext of disentangling her necklace from a creeper at the time of her departure, and similarly Śakuntalā delays her going away on the pretext that her foot is pricked by a thorn and her garment entangled in a branch. The heroines of both the plays write love-letters to their lovers.

In the delineation of the maddening grief of King Purūravas at Urvaśī's disappearance in Act IV of the Vik., Kālidāsa seems to have drawn inspiration from Vālmīki's *Rāmāyaṇa* which depicts Rāma as overwhelmed with grief at Sītā's disappearance, and as enquiring from trees and animals the whereabouts of Sītā.[7]

In the opening scene of Act I following the Prologue, a number of heavenly nymphs are seen piteously crying for help. King Purūravas who is returning after sun-worship rushes to help them. He is told by the nymph Rambhā that her friend Urvaśī, the gem of heaven, has been abducted by a demon, and that another nymph Chitralekhā is also with her. The King pursues the demon, rescues Urvaśī together with her companion, and brings her back in an unconscious state in the arms of Chitralekhā. On regaining consciousness when Urvaśī sees her saviour Purūravas, she falls in love with him at first sight. He is also charmed by her ravishing beauty. In the meantime, the Gandharva king Chitraratha, who was deputed by Indra to rescue Urvaśī, arrives there, thanks Purūravas, and takes Urvaśī to heaven. She is so much enamoured of Purūravas that at the time of her departure for heaven she turns back to have a glimpse of him on the pretext that she is disentangling her necklace entangled in a creeper. Then the King returns home with Urvaśī's deep love treasured in his heart.

Act II opens with an Interlude in which the King reveals his love for Urvaśī to the Jester and instructs him to keep it a secret. However, the Queen Auśīnarī's maid-servant Nipuṇikā, who is deputed by the Queen to find out the cause of the King's absent-mindedness since his return from the sunworship, cleverly extracts the secret from the Jester and reports it to the Queen.

In the scene following the Interlude the love-sick King and the Jester appear on the stage. After holding some conversation, both of them go to the pleasure-garden. The King asks the Jester to think out a plan for the former's union with Urvaśī, and the Jester feigns concentration to think out a plan. In the meantime, Urvaśī invisibly appears in the sky with her friend Chitralekhā, hears the King's lamentation that Urvaśī does not know his agony, and responds to it by dropping before him a love-letter written on birch-bark. On reading Urvaśī's love-letter the King is overjoyed and hands it over to the Jester for safe custody. Then Urvaśī preceded by Chitralekhā makes herself visible before the King and takes her seat with him after a brief exchange of greetings and amorous glances. But immediately thereafter she is recalled to heaven through a messenger to play a role in a drama to be enacted there. Urvaśī becomes sad and reluctantly takes leave of his sweet-heart. When the King asks the Jester to return the love-letter entrusted to him, the King is shocked to learn that the Jester has carelessly dropped it somewhere. Both start a frantic search for the letter which was blown away by wind and picked up by Nipuṇikā who read out its contents to the Queen. She flies into a rage on hearing its contents, goes to the King who is busy in search of the letter, tauntingly tells him about the recovery of the lost letter, and upbraids him for his love-affair. He falls at her feet and begs her forgiveness. But she is unreconciled and walks away in anger.

In the Prelude to Act III we are informed through a conversation between two pupils of the sage Bharata that during the performance of a play entitled *Lakṣmīsvayaṃvara* composed by Sarasvatī, when Menakā acting as Vāruṇī asked Urvaśī playing the role of Lakṣmī as to which of the assembled personages of the three worlds including Keśava and the guardians of the world had won her heart, she unconsciously replied "*Purūravas*" instead of "*Puruṣottama*" on account of her infatuation with Purūravas; that the sage Bharata angrily cursed her to lose her celestial status for committing this lapse; and that Indra intervened and favourably amended the curse to allow Urvaśī to dwell on earth with her lover Purūravas till such time as he would not see the face of his offspring born of her.

After the Prelude the scene opens in the evening with the entry of the chamberlain who has been sent by the Queen to invite the King to the terrace of the crystal palace to join her in the celebration of the Moon's union with the constellation Rohiṇī. In response to her invitation the King accompanied by the Jester goes to the terrace, and talks to him in private about his (King's) pangs of love. In the meantime, Urvaśī clad in a lovely dress arrives there in an aerial car with her friend Chitralekhā, and stands unseen (due to her supernatural powers) near the King and the Jester to eavesdrop their conversation. The Queen also arrives there with her retinue and receives due regard and courtesy from the King. Urvaśī feels a bit perturbed at it, but her fears are allayed by Chitralekhā. The Queen first offers her worship to the Moon, and then she worships the King and vows facing the Moon with folded hands: "With the pair of the Moon and Rohiṇī as my witnesses I hereby propitiate my lord, and take the vow that henceforth I shall amicably live with any woman whom my lord loves or chooses as his consort." After the Queen's exit Urvaśī approaches the King from behind and closes his eyes with her hands. Both are overjoyed at this happy meeting. Then Chitralekhā requests the King to make her friend so happy that she may not miss heaven. After emotionally embracing Urvaśī and respectfully greeting Purūravas, Chitralekhā leaves for heaven. The King holds Urvaśī's hand and retires to his room with her.

In the beginning of Act IV there is an Interlude in which

distressed Chitralekhā talks to another nymph Sahajanyā about the calamity that befell Urvaśī and Purūravas as narrated below. Once Urvaśī and Purūravas went to the Gandhamādana forest on the peak of Mount Kailāsa to enjoy amorous sports. One day she became angry with him on the suspicion that he was lustfully looking at a Vidyādhara girl, Udayavatī, playing on the bank of the Mandākinī. Enraged Urvaśī spurned all entreaties and supplications of the King, entered in a huff the god Kārttikeya's penance-grove prohibited to women, and was immediately transformed into a creeper. Chitralekhā adds that since then the King has been frantically searching Urvaśī everywhere day and night, and the appearance of clouds in the rainy season will further aggravate his agony.

In the scene following the Interlude the King appears like an insane person. He madly looks at a cloud and shouts, accusing it of stealing his beloved. He roams about in the forest and implores trees, creepers, birds, beasts, and even a mountain peak to tell him the whereabouts of his beloved. He fancies Urvaśī transformed into a mountain stream and imagines its waves as the knitting of her eye-brows, the rows of agitated birds as her girdle, the streaks of foam as her garment loosened in anger, and the meandering current as the stumbling gait of her jealous beloved.[8] He senselessly dances, sings, cries, faints and imagines the echo of the mountain to be a reply to his query. In the course of his wanderings he curiously picks up a red gem but throws it away. At that time he is advised by a divine voice (supposed to be the voice of Lord Śiva) to take back the *Saṅgamanīya* gem which will bring about his reunion with Urvaśī. Then he again picks up the gem and embraces a flowerless creeper which immediately turns into Urvaśī. They are overjoyed at their reunion and return to the Capital. Act IV is mostly lyrical.

The Prelude to Act V opens with the soliloquy of the Vidūṣaka who informs us that the King after his return from the Gandhamādana forest is having a happy time with Urvaśī and is reigning well to the full satisfaction of his subjects; that he has nothing to worry about except the lack of offspring; and that he has today gone to the confluence of the rivers Gaṅgā and Yamunā for a holy bath in the company of his Queen.

Suddenly there is an announcement behind the curtain that the *Saṅgamanīya* gem has been carried away by a vulture, mistaking it for a piece of meat. The Vidūṣaka expresses his sorrow and decides to go to the King.

In the scene following the Prelude the King, who enters the stage with his charioteer, an archer and attendants, sees the vulture hovering around, and asks for his bow and arrows. But the vulture disappears before the King could use his weapon. Soon thereafter the chamberlain enters with the gem and an arrow inscribed with the legend "the arrow of Āyus, son of Urvaśī and Purūravas". The King is delighted to recover the gem, but is amazed at the legend inscribed on the arrow. In the meantime, an old female ascetic comes there with a youth and informs the King that the boy was entrusted by his mother Urvaśī to the sage Chyavana who brought up and educated him at his hermitage, but the boy is now returned to his mother because he has violated the rule of the hermitage by killing a bird with his arrow. Urvaśī, who is called there to reveal the truth, feels shocked at the thought of her imminent separation from the King, because she has to return to heaven in accordance with Indra's stipulation that as soon as the King sees his offspring the period of her stay on earth would come to an end. Gloom spreads everywhere and the King decides to renounce the world after handing over the kingdom to his son. At that time a heartening message is brought from heaven by Nārada who tells the King that, since Indra needs the help of Purūravas against the demons, he (Indra) wants him to continue as King and has allowed Urvaśī to stay with him for good. There are scenes of jubilation everywhere. Prince Āyus is installed as Heir Apparent. Thus the play ends on a happy note.

Pūrūravas is depicted by Kālidāsa as a chivalrous and modest hero, valiant king, passionate lover, considerate husband and affectionate father. On hearing the news of Urvaśī's abduction, he immediately rushes to her help, but shows his modesty when his valour is praised by the Gandharva king Chitraratha. Indra values the prowess of Purūravas who is reputed to have rendered great help to the gods in their fight against demons. In appreciation of his valour Indra grants him permanent union with Urvaśī. The character of Purūravas as a passionate lover is vividly portrayed in the play. He falls in love with Urvaśī at first sight, and pines for her till their union. The grief of Urvaśī's separation turns him mad as shown in Act IV. He decides to renounce the world when he is again confronted with the grim prospect of his permanent separation from her. He is considerate to his first Queen Auśīnarī and even falls at her feet to conciliate her when she upbraids him after getting hold of Urvaśī's love-letter. As soon as he meets his son Āyus, Purūravas pours out his paternal affection on him and later instals him as Heir Apparent.

The character of Urvaśī, who is painted as a heartless nymph in the Vedic mythology, has been considerably improved by Kālidāsa in this play. She is depicted in the play as possessed of celestial beauty but earthly love. She falls in love with Purūravas at first sight and is so much enamoured of him that she unconsciously utters his name instead of "Puruṣottama" in her dramatic role. Her passionate love for Purūravas is full of jealousy which erupts at the slightest suspicion—on the King's expression of formal courtesy for the Queen Auśīnarī in Act III and on his sighting a Vidyādhara girl in Act IV. Urvaśī is nowhere shown as expressing her motherly affection towards her son Āyus whom she left in a hermitage immediately after his birth with a view to preventing her separation from Purūravas. It appears to be a common trait of nymphal character; for, Śakuntalā was also abandoned by her mother Menakā immediately after her birth. Kālidāsa has sought to blend both nymphal and human traits in the character of Urvaśī.

Queen Auśīnarī is portrayed as a dignified, sober and magnanimous lady who commands the respect and admiration of the King. Although she first gives vent to her natural anger at the unfaithful behaviour of her husband and severely rebukes him on the discovery of Urvaśī's love-letter, on cool consideration she changes her attitude and takes a solemn vow at the time of celebrating the Moon's union with Rohiṇī that she would gladly put up with any woman whom the King loves. Even Urvaśī praises Auśīnarī's grace and dignity as Queen.

The Vidūṣaka, who acts as a companion and confidant of

the King, is a comic character. He entertains the audience not only with his humorous and witty remarks but also with his stupid behaviour. When the King asks him to suggest a place of recreation, he promptly suggests him to go to the royal kitchen full of delicious preparations. On account of his fondness for sweets he fancies the rising Moon as a sweet ball, and describes heaven as a boring place without foods and drinks where the celestial beings live like fish with unwinking eyes. He gullibly blurts out before the Queen's maid-servant Nipuṇikā the King's secret of his love-affair with Urvaśī. Similarly the Vidūṣaka puts Purūravas in a very embarrassing position by carelessly dropping Urvaśī's love-letter entrusted to him by the King.

The Abhijñāna-Śākuntala

The chief characteristic of the play is expressed by its very title *Abhijñāna-Śākuntala*, which literally means a play in which its heroine Śakuntalā is recognized or recollected through a token. Moreover, the title testifies to Kālidāsa's richness of imagination in transforming a simple and crude Epic tale into a unique play of unsurpassed excellence. Kālidāsa has displayed his ingenuity and skill in the construction of the plot by making some important changes in the Epic version of the story and by introducing several new situations and incidents into it. In the Mahābhārata[9] Śakuntalā is shown as a dauntless rustic girl who herself tells Duṣyanta the story of her birth, argues with him about the legality of secret union, stipulates a condition for marriage, and rebukes him in his court for repudiating her. Moreover, in the Epic version Śakuntalā goes to Duṣyanta's court with a child, and Duṣyanta tells a blatant lie that he does not recognize her. Kālidāsa has removed all these crudities of the story by inventing the episodes of curse and the loss of the ring. Besides, in the play Śakuntalā is shown as enceinte at the time of her arrival in Duṣyanta's court, and the reunion of the separated lovers takes place in the hermitage of the sage Mārīcha after a long period of suffering and purification, whereas the Epic hero initially refuses to recognize Śakuntalā but later accepts her together with her son in the court itself on the intervention of a heavenly voice.

As we have pointed out above, some important points of similarity between the Vik. and the Śak. indicate that the former is a precursor of the latter in which Kālidāsa's dramatic art has reached its zenith. The Śak. which has won universal admiration reveals the ingenuity of Kālidāsa's creative genius and the perfection of his art in the construction of the plot, in characterisation, in the delineation of pathos and love, in the description of Nature, in poetic justice, and in the simplicity, elegance and felicity of expression. In the Śak. Kālidāsa has tempered the passions of love and pathos and kept them within aesthetic limits. Sir Monier Williams has aptly summed up the admirable qualities of the Śak. in the following words: "No composition of Kālidāsa displays more the richness of his poetical genius, the exuberance of his imagination, the warmth and play of his fancy, his profound knowledge of the human heart, his delicate appreciation of its most refined and tender emotions, his familiarity with the workings and counter-workings of its conflicting feelings,—in short, more entitles him to rank as the Shakespeare of India."

An English translation of the epigram composed by the German poet Goethe in praise of the Śak. has already been given above in Chapter I.

The play opens with the Prologue in which obeisance is paid to Lord Śiva in the opening stanza, the play and its author are introduced, and a verse each is sung by the stage-manager and his wife to express the charms of pleasant and delightful days of enjoyable Summer. Appreciating his wife's song and hinting at the ensuing scene of the play, the stage-manager tells his wife in a verse that his mind has been swayed by the fascinating melody of her song, just as King Duṣyanta has been carried away by his pursuit of a fleeting gazelle.

After the Prologue King Duṣyanta, mounted on a chariot, is shown as pursuing a gazelle who is running at a neckbreak speed, and whose path is strewn with half-chewed blades of Darbha grass dropped from his mouth opened in fatigue. When the King is about to discharge an arrow at the gazelle in the vicinity of a hermitage, he hears the loud voices of hermits dissuading him from killing the gazelle who belongs to the hermitage. In compliance with their request the King withdraws his arrow and pays respects to the hermits who bless him with the birth of a sovereign son and who invite him to accept their hospitality in the sage Kaṇva's hermitage situated on the bank of the river Mālinī. The King learns from them that the sage Kaṇva has gone to Somatīrtha to ward off an impending misfortune of his daughter Śakuntalā, after having entrusted her with the duty of offering hospitality to guests. Leaving behind his chariot and retinue, the King alone enters the hermitage, and sights there three girls carrying pitchers to water plants. He stands unseen by them in the shade of a tree, carefully observes them, overhears their conversation, feels fascinated by the ravishing beauty of Śakuntalā dressed in a bark-garment, and speculates on her suitability as his bride on account of her birth. When Śakuntalā is harassed by a bee and cries for help, her friends tell her in joke to invoke the help of King Duṣyanta. On hearing all this, the King suddenly appears before them and enquires about the cause of their panic. They tell him that their friend Śakuntalā was frightened by a bee. The matter is laughed away, and the King is invited by them to take a seat. The girls also sit there. When Śakuntalā's companion Anasūyā asks Duṣyanta about his family, birth-place and the purpose of his visit, he introduces himself in an equivocal phrase which can be interpreted to mean "a royal officer in charge of religious affairs" or "King Duṣyanta" on a visit to the hermitage to ascertain the unhindered performance of religious activities.[10] Then he enquires about Śakuntalā's parentage from her friends who inform him that she is the daughter of the nymph Menakā and the sage Viśvāmitra, and that her foster-father Kaṇva wants a suitable match for her. Śakuntalā, who falls in love with the King at first sight, feels shy at their conversation about her, feigns anger and pretends to leave the place. Her friends prevent her from going away, and the King observes the blush of love on her face. In the meantime it is announced that a wild elephant, frightened by the King's hunting party, is menacing the hermitage. On hearing this news, the girls are perturbed and go to their residence. But in order to have a glimpse of Duṣyanta love-smitten Śakuntalā tarries for a while on the pretext of removing a pointed blade of Darbha grass from her foot, and disentangling her garment from the branches of trees.

In the beginning of Act II the dejected Jester Māṭhavya grumbles about the hardships suffered by him during Duṣyanta's hunting excursion, nostalgically recalls the comforts of city life, and regrets that the King is so much enamoured of Śakuntalā that he never thinks of returning to the Capital. In the meantime, the King arrives there accompanied by Greek (*Yavana*) girls as attendants who bear bows in their hands and wear the garlands of flowers. He orders his men to stop hunting on account of the proximity of the hermitage. Then Duṣyanta talks to Māṭhavya in confidence about the ravishing beauty of Śakuntalā and expresses his (Duṣyanta's) deep love for her, but the Jester talks in a lighter vein. While they are thinking of a pretext to visit the hermitage, two ascetic youths approach the King with a request from the hermits to protect the hermitage for a few nights from demons who disturb sacrifices in the absence of the sage Kaṇva. The King gladly accepts their request, sends the Jester to the Capital to represent him (Duṣyanta) at a religious ceremony to be performed by Queen Mother in compliance with a message received from her, and tells Māṭhavya not to take seriously his (King's) light-hearted remarks about his love for Śakuntalā.

In the Prelude to Act III a pupil of the sage Kaṇva praises Duṣyanta for affording protection from demons, and informs us that Śakuntalā's companions are worried about her sickness caused by exposure to the sun and are doing their best to cure her, as she is the very life-breath of the sage Kaṇva.

In the scene following the Prelude the love-sick King pines for Śakuntalā, and addresses verses to Cupid, blaming him for tormenting him through the moon and flowers. As he moves about restlessly, he sights love-smitten Śakuntalā lying in an arbour on a stone-slab covered with flowers. Her two companions, Priyaṃvadā and Anasūyā, who are fanning her with lotus-leaves, jocularly tell her that her sickness is not physical but mental due to her deep love for the King. She confesses her love and writes a love-letter to him on a lotus-leaf at their suggestion. The King, who has overheard their confidential conversation, appears suddenly before them and says that not only Śakuntalā but he is also tormented by love. Śakuntalā stands up and he sits on the stone-slab. Her friend Priyaṃvadā requests the King to save the life of Śakuntalā languishing in love for him. But Śakuntalā tells Priyaṃvadā not to detain the King who must be very anxious to return to his harem on account of his long absence from there. But the King remonstrates and makes protestations of his deep love exclusively for her. Anasūyā tells him that, as the kings have many wives, Śakuntalā should not be maltreated in his harem. The King assures them that despite his many wives Śakuntalā would enjoy a pre-eminent position in his household. Then her two friends retire from there on some pretext, leaving the lovers together. Śakuntalā also wants to go away, but she is held back by him. Then they enter into a secret matrimonial alliance, after Duṣyanta persuades her to marry him on the plea that secret union is permissible under the *Gāndharva* form of marriage (see Note 28a of Chapter VII) which was adopted in the past by numerous Kṣatriya maidens and later approved by their parents. A voice from behind the curtain informs them of the arrival of the female ascetic Gautamī. The King hides behind the trees, and Śakuntalā quits the place with Gautamī.

Act IV opens with an Interlude in which Śakuntalā's two friends, Anasūyā and Priyaṃvadā, who were plucking flowers for worship, talk about the secret union of Śakuntalā and Duṣyanta and express their anxiety about her future lest the King, who has since returned to his Capital, should forget her. In the meantime, her two friends first hear a voice announcing the arrival of a guest in the hermitage during Śakuntalā's absent-mindedness owing to her absorption in love; and then they are shocked to hear the voice of the short-tempered sage Durvāsas who angrily curses Śakuntalā[11] : "O insolent lady ! he in whose thought you are lost will forget you and will not recall you, even when he is reminded, like a deranged person, since you disregard a sage, like me, present before you." Priyaṃvadā rushes to the sage Durvāsas and pleads with him to forgive their friend, as it is her first fault. He relents a bit and says that the King would recognize her when some ornament is shown to him as a token of recognition. As the King had presented Śakuntalā with his signet ring inscribed with his name as a memento at the time of his departure, her friends are satisfied that it would ward off the evil effect of the curse.

In the scene following the Interlude a pupil of the sage Kaṇva describes the morning scene marked by the setting of the Moon and the rise of the Sun, and thus hints at the rise and fall of fortune in life. Then Anasūyā arrives there and laments that the King has been very unfair to Śakuntalā and that it is now difficult to communicate to the sage Kaṇva the news of her approaching maternity. Just then Priyaṃvadā comes there and asks Anasūyā to make preparations for the farewell of Śakuntalā who is being sent by the sage Kaṇva to the Capital that very day, as on his return to the hermitage he learnt from a heavenly voice about Śakuntalā's secret marriage with Duṣyanta and her approaching maternity. The entire hermitage is agog with preparations for bidding farewell to Śakuntalā. Here Kālidāsa displays the richness of his poetic imagination in delineating human sentiments. He vividly describes here how Śakuntalā's two friends and her foster-father sage Kaṇva express their anguish at her impending departure, and how emotionally she takes leave of her friends, foster-father, pet fawn, plants and creepers of the hermitage. Moreover, the playwright imaginatively describes Nature in full sympathy with human sentiments. The sylvan deities offer garments and ornaments for the decoration of Śakuntalā; birds bid her farewell in sweet sounds; and the animals and creepers also give vent to their grief on the occasion of her departure. Her two friends, Priyaṃvadā and Anasūyā, collect necessary materials such as yellow pigment, sprouts, and flowers for her decoration, and rush to Śakuntalā who has already taken her bath and is receiving blessings from female ascetics holding the auspicious grains of wild rice in their hands. Her two friends congratulate Śakuntalā, and set about the novel task of adorning her with the simple materials brought by them, but regret that her peerless beauty worthy of precious ornaments is slighted by decoration with such toiletry as is available in the hermitage. At that very moment two hermit youths enter the stage with precious presents in their hands, and announce that Śakuntalā should be adorned with these ornaments. All are amazed at it. The youths explain that, when they approached trees for flowers in compliance with the command of the sage Kaṇva, an auspicious silken garment as white as the moon was offered by one tree, liquid lac-dye for painting feet was presented by another, and ornaments were given by the sylvan deities with their sprout-like tender hands revealed up to the wrists from other trees.[12] Priyaṃvadā and Anasūyā adorn Śakuntalā with these ornaments, saying that though they have got no practical knowledge of wearing ornaments, yet they would arrange them on her body as observed by them in paintings. Then the sage Kaṇva enters the stage and expresses his deep anguish at the thought of Śakuntalā's separation from him[13] : "At the thought of Śakuntalā's imminent departure today my heart is full of sorrow, my throat is chocked with tears, and my senses are numbed by anxiety. If such be the sorrow of an anchorite like me on account of her affection, how much more are householders not grieved at the fresh separation of their own daughters from them ?" Śakuntalā bashfully pays her respect to the sage who bestows blessings on her. After she has circumambulated the sacrificial Fires, the sage pronounces benediction for her, signals her departure, and addresses the trees to bid her farewell. A cukco's note coming from the grove is taken as the farewell message of the trees. An incorporeal voice, which is supposed to be uttered by the sylvan deities, wishes her a happy and comfortable journey. The agony of separation is felt not only by Śakuntalā but also by the entire hermitage. Feeling sad at Śakuntalā's imminent separation, the female deer have dropped the morsels of *darbha* grass from their mouths, the peacocks have ceased dancing, and the creepers appear to shed tears in the form of pale leaves.[14] Śakuntalā bids tearful farewell to the jasmine creeper and the fawn reared by her, and departs weeping. All accompany her up to a lake where they stand in the shade of a tree. Then the sage asks Śārṅgarava, one of his pupils who will escort Śakuntalā, to convey his message to Duṣyanta that he should treat her at par with his other wives, keeping in view the sage's ascetic life, Duṣyanta's own noble family, and her spontaneous love for him without the prompting of her relatives; and that the rest depends upon her luck which should not be said by her relatives.[15] At the same time the sage advises Śakuntalā to serve her elders, to treat her co-wives as her dear friends, to refrain from doing anything against her husband in anger even when she is wronged by him, to be magnanimous with her servants, to eschew arrogance in prosperity, and to remember that maidens thus attain the status of mistress of the house but those who behave perversely become the bane of the family.[16] Śakuntalā affectionately embraces the sage and touches his feet. Then her two friends embrace her simultaneously and suggest that if the King hesitates to recognize her she should show him the signet ring presented by him. Facing the hermitage, she asks the sage as to when she will again see the hermitage. The sage replies that she will visit the peaceful hermitage in the company of her husband, after having enjoyed for a long time the position of Chief Queen and having entrusted to her son the administration of the kingdom. Escorted by the old ascetic lady Gautamī and the sage's two pupils, Śakuntalā leaves for the Capital. When their party is out of sight, the sage Kaṇva, Priyaṃvadā and Anasūyā return to the hermitage.

In the opening scene of Act V King Duṣyanta and the Vidūṣaka are shown as sitting and listening to a melodious voice coming from the music hall. They soon realize that Haṃsapadikā, one of the queens, is singing a song describing metaphorically the King's indifferent attitude towards her. Duṣyanta sends the Vidūṣaka to tell Haṃsapadikā that he (Duṣyanta) has understood the taunt implied in her song. After the Jester's exit the chamberlain informs the King about the arrival of two hermits accompanied by two ladies with a message from the sage Kaṇva. The King orders that the chaplain Somarāta should be asked to offer due hospitality to the guests and to bring them to the Fire-sanctuary where he (the King) will be waiting for them. Accordingly Śakuntalā, Gautamī and two hermits are led by the chamberlain and the chaplain to the Fire-sanctuary. Although Śakuntalā's face is covered with a veil, yet the King is fascinated by the charming beauty of her form. After preliminary courtesies are over, the sage Kaṇva's pupil, Śārṅgarava, delivers the sage's message that he has gladly approved the marriage, contracted by Duṣyanta with Śakuntalā due to mutual agreement, and that

Śakuntalā who is now in a family way should be accepted by him as his wife. Duṣyanta expresses his amazement at this message and denies his marriage with Śakuntalā. Gautamī removes Śakuntalā's veil for the King to recognize her. After casting a glance at her face, the King tacitly admires her ravishing beauty and likens his own helplessness in the matter to that of a bee which can neither enjoy nor give up a jasmine flower soaked in dew in the morning.[17] Duṣyanta asks Śakuntalā to convince him about her marriage with him. In order to dispel his doubts she decides to show him the signet ring as token of recognition, but is stunned to find her finger without the ring. When the King ridicules her attempt as feminine cunningness, she retorts that he, who under the garb of righteousness is like a well covered with grass, judges others by the standard of his own heart. She covers her face with her garment and weeps. Śārṅgarava rebukes the King and finally says to him: "Here is your wife. Accept her or repudiate her, because the husband has got full authority over his wife." When the two hermits and Gautamī leave the place, Śakuntalā follows them. But Śārṅgarava angrily turns back and scolds her, saying that they cannot take her back to the hermitage. She trembles with fear and does not know what to do. Duṣyanta consults the royal chaplain who suggests that she could stay in his (chaplain's) house till her delivery and could be accepted by the King if she gives birth to a son with the marks of sovereignty in accordance with the prediction, otherwise she would be sent back. Śakuntalā goes out with the chaplain and the hermits, crying "O Goddess Earth ! take me into your bosom." The chaplain returns after a short while, and tells the King that on the departure of Kaṇva's pupils when she began to cry piteously blaming her fate she was lifted up by a heavenly light, resembling the figure of a woman, which went to the lake of nymphs (*apsaras-tīrtha*). Duṣyanta evinces no interest in the incident, feels perturbed, and retires to bed.

In the Prelude to Act VI the city Superintendent of Police enters with two police constables and an accused with his hands tied behind. The constables thrash him and enquire from him as to how he obtained the royal signet ring which he was trying to dispose of. The accused who is a fisherman residing in the vicinity of the *Śakrāvatāra Tīrtha* tells them that he found it in the belly of a fish. The Superintendent goes to the King with the ring and soon returns with a big reward awarded by the King to the fisherman who shares it with his captors to save his skin. The Superintendent tells his companions that the King highly values the ring not for its costly gem but for the fact that on its sight he was reminded of a very dear person and appeared to be remorseful for a moment.

In the scene following the Prelude the nymph Sānumatī, sent by Śakuntalā's mother Menakā to know the state of affairs in Duṣyanta's household, descends from the sky and finds no festivities in the royal household on the advent of vernal season. Remaining unseen through her supernatural powers, she overhears the conversation of two female guards of the royal garden, who pluck mango blossoms and worship Kāmadeva, the god of love, with them. But they are then rebuked by the chamberlain for defying the royal orders, because the King has banned the celebration of vernal festival on account of his remorse at the wrongful repudiation of his dear wife Śakuntalā. The chamberlain further informs the female guards, who are new-comers in the Capital, that ever since the recovery of the signet ring the King has been passing restless nights, and that he is emaciated on account of his agony. In the next scene the King arrives in the garden along with the Jester and opens his heart to him about his (King's) miserable condition resulting from his repudiation of Śakuntalā. He asks his female door-keeper to tell the minister that, as he (King) is unable to attend the royal court of justice due to his wakefulness at night, the minister should officiate for him and submit his judgements in writing to the King. In compliance with the King's orders another female attendant brings to him a picture of Śakuntalā painted by him. He discusses with the Jester some points of the picture and asks the maid-servant to fetch the brush and colours, because he has to give the finishing touch to the picture. While the King and the Jester talk about the picture and the former expresses his anguish at Śakuntalā's repudiation, the maid-servant returns and reports that Queen Vasumatī, who has snatched the painting material from her hand, is coming to the King. He hands over the picture to the Jester who goes away with it. After the Jester's exit the female door-keeper enters with a written message from the minister and informs the King that the Queen, who was coming to him, has returned back after seeing the important documents in her (door-keeper's) hand. The King says that the Queen does not want to disturb him in the discharge of his royal duties. The King receives his minister's report that on the death of a childless rich merchant named Dhanamitra in a ship-wreck his property escheats to the Crown. On reading this report, the King expresses his sorrow at childlessness and issues orders to find out if any of his (dead merchant's) wives is in a family way. When the King is told by the door-keeper that one of his wives is expecting a child, he orders that the child in the womb shall be entitled to inherit the paternal property. Then he laments his own childlessness, and regrets the repudiation of his wife Śakuntalā who was to bear him an offspring. Pondering over it, he becomes unconscious; and the nymph Sānumatī, who has been secretly watching so far the King's actions, returns to heaven to report this news to Śakuntalā to reassure her of Duṣyanta's deep love for her. On regaining consciousness, the King hears the piteous cries of the Jester and rushes to his help. Duṣyanta is puzzled, as he is unable to see Indra's charioteer Mātali who has seized the Jester to provoke the King's anger and thus to divert his mind. When Duṣyanta fits an arrow to the bow-string, Mātali leaves the Jester and appears before the King to deliver to him Indra's message in which Duṣyanta is requested to accompany Mātali in the divine chariot to help Indra in exterminating a host of formidable demons born of Kālanemi. The King decides to accompany Mātali and conveys his decision to his minister through the Jester. Then Duṣyanta mounts the divine chariot and leaves for heaven with Mātali.

The final Act of the play culminates into the happy reunion of Duṣyanta and Śakuntalā. In the opening scene the King is shown as returning to earth from heaven in Indra's chariot with Mātali after vanquishing demons. Mātali lauds Duṣyanta's modesty with regard to his valour, while the latter thanks Indra for the honours bestowed upon him in heaven. In the course of their descent from heaven to earth the King is delighted by the spectacular sight presented by the earth, and he vividly describes it as viewed from the flying chariot. When Mātali informs the King about their flight over the Hemakūṭa mountain where the hermitage of the sage Mārīcha is situated, the King expresses his desire to visit the hermitage to pay respects to the revered sage. Mātali lands the chariot in the hermitage, and both of them alight from it. Mātali goes to the sage Mārīcha to secure an appointment for the King who himself waits for Mātali's return under an Aśoka tree. Duṣyanta feels the throbbing of his right arm which augurs good luck. He sights a small boy who forcibly drags a sucking lion cub from its mother to play with. Two ascetic ladies, who try to dissuade the boy from this dangerous play, talk about him and remark that he has been appropriately named *Sarvadamana*, "subduer of all", by the sages. One of them asks the boy to leave the lion cub for a toy. The boy stretches out his hand for the promised toy and insists on playing with the lion cub till he gets a toy. The lady goes away to fetch a toy. The King feels unconsciously attracted by the boy and sees the marks of sovereignty on his palm. The other ascetic lady requests the King to prevent the boy from dragging the lion cub. When the King releases the lion cub from the boy's grip and holds him in his arms, he feels the delight of paternal affection towards him. The ascetic lady is amazed at the close resemblance between the boy and the King, and tells him that the boy hails from the *Puru* family but she would not utter the name of his father who repudiated his lawful wife. The lady, who had gone to fetch a toy, comes back with a peacock toy in her hand, and tells the boy: "Sarvadamana ! look at the beauty of the bird" (*Śakuntalāvaṇyam*)." By mixing in confusion the first member (*śakunta*) of the compound with the initial syllable (*lā*) of the following word (*lāvaṇyam*) due to the similarity of sound, the boy eagerly asks her as to where his mother (*Śakuntalā*) is. The King wonders if he is the son of Śakuntalā. When the King picks up without any harm to himself the talisman that had slipped down from the boy's wrist, the two ladies are struck with wonder, because if any person other than the boy or his parents were to touch the talisman it would at once turn into a snake and bite that person. Both the ladies go to Śakuntalā to apprise her of Duṣyanta's arrival, while the King caresses *Sarvadamana*, addressing him as his son. But the boy tells him : "No, you are not my father. My father is Duṣyanta".

In the meantime, emaciated Śakuntalā arrives there, wearing a pair of faded garments, keeping her hair tied in a single knot, and observing the pure conduct of a chaste wife separated from her husband.[18] The King at once rocognizes her and expresses his delight. She also recognizes Duṣyanta and greets him in a voice choked with tears: "Victory to my lord". The King falls at her feet and begs her forgiveness, but she requests him to get up and blames her own previous deeds for her miseries. The King narrates to her the incident about the recovery of the ring and its magic effect in reviving his past memories of their love. He offers her the ring, but she declines to accept it on the plea that she no longer trusts it. Duṣyanta and Śakuntalā accompanied by their son Sarvadamana go to the sage Mārīcha, who is sitting with his wife Aditi, and pay their respects to both of them. In order to remove their remorse and doubts the sage tells them that the curse of Durvāsas was solely responsible for clouding the King's memory which was later revived by the sight of the recovered ring. The sage Mārīcha bestows blessings on the reunited pair, sends one of his pupils to the sage Kaṇva to apprise him of their happy reunion, and bids them farewell on their return journey to the Capital in Indra's chariot. The play concludes with a benedictory stanza called *Bharatavākya*.

Characterisation in the Śak. is of a very high order. All the characters ranging from the sage Kaṇva to the policemen have been vividly portrayed. Kālidāsa has removed the blemish of falsehood and faithlessness from Duṣyanta's character through the device of curse and the loss of the signet ring.

King Duṣyanta in the play stands out as a righteous and benevolent ruler, valiant hero, polished gentleman, sincere lover and affectionate father. He at once withdraws his arrow aimed at the deer on the intervention of the hermits and shows due regard to the sanctity of the hermitage. He believes that one-sixth of the holy merit earned by the hermits accrues to the king for affording protection to them. He regularly holds his court to deal out justice to his subjects and himself supervises the decrees passed by his minister. The minister had decided that the property of the issueless merchant Dhanamitra deceased in a ship-wreck should escheat to the Crown. But King Duṣyanta revises the judgement, orders an enquiry about the merchant's offspring, and decrees that the progeny in the womb of one of his widows shall inherit his property. The King issues the proclamation that if any of his subjects lose their dear relatives Duṣyanta would represent them except in a sinful relationship. His conscience does not allow him to take a peerless beauty like Śakuntalā to his harem when he is unable to recall his marriage with her due to the curse, though he is fascinated by her ravishing beauty. He deems it the duty of a king to bear patiently all strains and stresses of administration for the welfare of his subjects. Duṣyanta is renowned for his valour, and even the god Indra seeks his aid in exterminating demons. Despite his valour Duṣyanta is sober and modest. He tells Mātali that though he (Duṣyanta) has carried out Indra's orders yet the great honour shown to him by the lord of heaven makes him feel that he is unworthy of it. He is a polished and courteous gentleman. Although he is severely rebuked by Śārṅgarava for repudiating Śakuntalā, Duṣyanta does not lose his temper in his imperial arrogance and does not utter any harsh words except in hurling the charge of feminine cunningness at Śakuntalā on her failure to show the signet ring. He is charmed by Śakuntalā's ravishing beauty at her first sight in the hermitage, but he sets his heart on her only after he has ascertained her suitability as his bride. Duṣyanta is a sincere lover who pines for his beloved and who does not show attachment to any woman other than Śakuntalā, though he is polygamous. When he recollects his love with Śakuntalā on the sight of the signet ring, he feels remorseful for repudiating her, suffers pangs of her separation, bans the celebration of the vernal festival, paints her picture, and loses his sleep in her thoughts. At the time of reunion he falls at her feet and begs her forgiveness. Duṣyanta's paternal affection unconsciously flows out, when he meets his son Sarvadamana in the hermitage and touches him for the first time.

The Vidūṣaka Māṭhavya is depicted in the Śak. as

Duṣyanta's companion and confidant. Duṣyanta opens his heart before him and shares his secrets with him. Māṭhavya detests the King's hunting excursion and recalls his easy life in the city. His remarks sometimes evoke laughter but also betray his pragmatism in certain situations. He often talks of food and is a coward who is easily frightened.

Kaṇva is portrayed as a pious, sagacious and kind-hearted sage who affectionately brought up Śakuntalā abandoned by her mother, and who visited Somatīrtha to ward off Śakuntalā's impending misfortune. He is shown as possessed of occult powers through which he learns of Śakuntalā's secret union with Duṣyanta. Although Kaṇva obliquely hints at the blind passion of Śakuntalā, he generously forgives her and approves of her secret marriage. In spite of his ascetic way of life he is deeply moved by Śakuntalā's affection at the time of her departure from the hermitage. Kaṇva's sagacity is reflected in his farewell advice to Śakuntalā and in his message conveyed to Duṣyanta.

Kālidāsa portrays Śakuntalā as a paragon of beauty and embodiment of virtues. King Duṣyanta employs superlatives to describe her ravishing beauty at her first sight and observes that such a celestial beauty cannot be born on earth. Her external beauty is matched by the excellent qualities of her head and heart. Although she falls in love with Duṣyanta at first sight, she agrees to marry him only after ascertaining that he also loves her ardently and that their secret union is lawful. She expresses her love to him in a love-letter written at the suggestion of her friends. She loves him so passionately that she remains absorbed in his thoughts and neglects her duty of offering hospitality to the sage Durvāsas. As a child of Nature Śakuntalā loves trees, creepers and animals of the hermitage besides her foster-father and two friends. At the time of her departure she expresses her profound grief at her impending separation from them. When King Duṣyanta repudiates her, she restrains her anger and does not argue with him nor does she rebuke him unlike the Śakuntalā of the *Mahābhārata*. Kālidāsa's Śakuntalā displays exemplary forbearance. However, she is constrained to retort when Duṣyanta accuses her of characteristic feminine cunningness on her failure to show the ring. In the hermitage of the sage Mārīcha she leads a life of austerity and self-restraint in keeping with the conduct of a chaste wife separated from her husband. When King Duṣyanta first meets her there, she does not blame him for her repudiation and holds her own previous deeds responsible for her miseries. She feels ashamed at the King's prostration before her. Śakuntalā is a peerless beauty, refined and decent lady and ideal wife. She is a fine blend of the good qualities of both heaven and earth.

Śakuntalā's two companions, who have been aptly christened by Kālidāsa as *Anasūyā* "free from malice" and *Priyaṃvadā* "sweet-tongued", are depicted as jovial, witty, sincere and affable maids. They cut jokes with her, understand her youthful feelings, and help her in her love-affair. When Śakuntalā confesses before them her love for Duṣyanta, they encourage her in her love and help the lovers in their secret union. In all the scenes Anasūyā and Priyaṃvadā appear together. Both of them express their anxiety about Śakuntalā's future when no news is received from Duṣyanta who at the time of his departure for his Capital had promised to take her to his harem in a few days. Both the maids jointly decorate Śakuntalā with ornaments, flowers, etc., and embrace her simnltaneously at the time of bidding her farewell. Although the character of Anasūyā is hardly distinguishable from that of Priyaṃvadā, the former is portrayed as more talkative than the latter. It is Anasūyā who questions Duṣyanta about his family, his birth-place and the purpose of his visit to the hermitage ; who tells him about Śakuntalā's parentage ; who extracts from Śakuntalā her confession of love for Duṣyanta ; and who requests the King to treat her friend kindly in his harem. Priyaṃvadā is depicted as more mature, shrewd and observant. She is quick to observe Duṣyanta's features as a great personality at first sight. She can judge from Duṣyanta's facial expression that he wants to say something. Pointing to Śakuntalā's love-sickness, Priyaṃvadā tells Anasūyā that their friend seems to have been excited ever since she first met Duṣyanta. Priyaṃvadā encourages Śakuntalā in her love for Duṣyanta by praising his qualities, suggests to her to write a love-letter to him, and observes that the King is also pining for Śakuntalā. On account of her shrewdness Priyaṃvadā is requested by Anasūyā to approach the irascible sage Durvāsas to seek his forgiveness for Śakuntalā's negligence in offering due hospitality to him ; and Priyaṃvadā succeeds to a large extent in persuading him to forgive Śakuntalā. Displaying her keen observation of Nature, Priyaṃvadā tells Śakuntalā that the feeling of imminent separation has saddened not only her but also the entire hermitage where female deer have dropped from their mouths the morsels of Darbha grass, the peacocks have stopped their dance, and the creepers seem to shed tears in the form of pale leaves (*see* Note 14). The two maids, Anasūyā and Priyaṃvadā, not only play an important role in the drama but also help in bringing out some essential features of Śakuntalā's character.

Notes and References

1. Śak. IV, 11; *see* Note 65 of Chapter VI.
2. Ragh. XIV, 69; *see* Note 62 of Chapter VI.
3. K.R. Pisharoti, *Journal of the Annamalai University*, II, No. 2, pp. 193 ff.
4. Māl. II. 3.
5. Geldner, *Vedische Studien*, I, pp. 243 ff.
6. Vik. V, 9; Śak. VII, 19.
7. R. III, 60.
8. Vik. IV, 52.
9. Mbh. I, 68-74. *The Bhāgavata-Purāṇa* (IX, 20) contains a short extract of the story of Śakuntalā. However, the version of the story of Śakuntalā contained in one recension of the *Padma-Purāṇa* (Bock III) agrees closely with that of the Śak., and some scholars are inclined to regard this Purāṇa as the source of Kālidāsa's play; cf. Winternitz, *A History of Indian Literature*, Vol. I, p. 540 and particularly f.n. 2 on this page. But the priority of the *Padma-Purāṇa* to the Śak. is untenable on several grounds, one of which is that the Ānandāśrama edition of the *Padma-Purāṇa* omits altogether the *Śakuntalopākhyāna*; cf. V.V. Mirashi, *Kālidāsa*, p. 306; Keith, *A History of Sanskrit Literature*, Preface, p. x; S.K.De, *A History of Sanskrit Literature*, Vol. I, p. 140, f.n. 2.

10. भवति ! यः पौरवेण राज्ञा धर्माधिकारे नियुक्तः सोऽहमविघ्नक्रियोपलम्भाय धर्मारण्यमिदमायातः ।

(Śak., p. 40)

11. Śak. IV, 1.
12. Ibid. IV, 4.
13. Ibid. IV, 5.
14. Ibid. IV, 11.
15. Ibid. IV, 16.
16. Ibid. IV, 17.
17. Ibid. V, 19.
18. Ibid. VII, 21; cf. R. V, 15, 25.

5

The Language, Style and Imagery of Kālidāsa

Kālidāsa is noted for simplicity, directness, clarity, elegance and felicity of expression. He carefully chooses simple words of ordinary sense and standard usage and skilfully arranges them into significant, suggestive and catchy phrases whether they are in prose or verse. Take, for instance, the following remark made by love-sick Duṣyanta on the sight of Śakuntalā attended by her two friends in an arbour in Act III of the Śak. : *aye, labdham netra-nirvāṇam* "Hey ! my eyes are blessed". Unlike the later Sanskrit poets, Kālidāsa does not use rare and obsolete vocables and complicated grammatical forms to show off his learning. He generally employs simple and easy finite verbs or participial forms concordant with appropriate nouns and adjectives. For instance, there is a very simple finite verb *asti* in the first hemistich of the KS., and the past participle form *sthitaḥ* in the second hemistich. Similarly such simple verbal forms as *asmi*, *gamiṣyāmi* and *asti* are employed in the second, third and fourth verses of Canto I of the Ragh. In several cases the construction of sentences is so simple that their meaning is absolutely clear without the use of a finite verb. We may cite, for instance, Kālidāsa's famous saying occurring in the Śak. (I, 19) : *satāṃ hi saṃdeha-padeṣu vastuṣu pramāṇam antaḥkaraṇa-pravṛtayaḥ* "In matters of doubt good men's dictate of conscience is their final authority." Examples of this type can be easily multiplied.

Kālidāsa employs short compounds generally consisting of two or three simple words, and avoids the use of long and complicated compounds. He is equally careful about the choice of simple secondary (*Taddhita*) forms. He is, on the whole, sparing in the use of secondary forms. It is a characteristic feature of his poetry that the sense of a stanza is generally complete and clear without reference to the preceding and following stanzas. However, there are a few exceptions to this rule here and there. See, for instance, verses 5-9 of the First Canto of the Ragh. constituting a single sentence. He avoids the use of words with harsh sounds, and thoughtfully chooses such words as produce tender and pleasing sound to harmonize with the aesthetic sentiments of love and pathos which are mainly delineated in his works. Therefore, Kālidāsa's language is characterized by an admirable harmony of sound and sense.

Kālidāsa's works present the best specimen of *Vaidarbha* style of composition which is highly praised by Daṇḍin and later writers on Sanskrit poetics.[1]

Kālidāsa's expression is characterized by the rare quality of significant suggestion. He chooses such words and phrases as express through significant suggestion all the relevant implications of the subject or the situation described in a few words. Unlike Bhavabhūti, Kālidāsa does not expend words on the elaboration of a subject nor does he constantly hammer a point. He is content with a well thought out brief suggestion which expresses the implied meaning more eloquently than a number of stanzas. He has complete command of Sanskrit and displays his mastery of its nuances and subtleties.

It is also a noteworthy feature of Kālidāsa's language that he names the characters, invented by him in his plays, in such a manner as to bring out clearly the outstanding traits of their character. For instance, the chief Queen of King Agnimitra in the Māl. is named *Dhāriṇī* to emphasize her virtues of patience, calmness and forgiveness. A maid-servant of the junior Queen Irāvatī in the same play displays the qualities of cleverness and sharpness to justify her name *Nipuṇikā*. The junior Queen who often flies into a rage like the goddess *Chaṇḍī* is given the name *Irāvatī* which is one of the synonyms of Chaṇḍī. Śakuntalā's friend *Priyaṃvadā* endears herself to all by her sweet and agreeable speech in keeping with her name, while the sage Kaṇva's pupil *Śārṅgarava* silences everybody with his shrill voice resembling the sound (*rava*) of a horny (*śārṅga*) musical instrument, or that of a bird named *śārṅga*. It is thus obvious that Kālidāsa assigns such names to the invented dramatic personae as denote their derivative sense. Moreover, he exhibits his fondness for suggesting the etymologies of several popular names and words. For instance, he attempts in his own ingenious manner the derivation of *kṣatra*, *Raghu*, *rājan*, *Rāma*, *Umā* and *Aparṇā*.[2]

Kālidāsa was not only a master of the Sanskrit language but he was also well versed in the rules of the Sanskrit grammar. Therefore, he displays his knowledge of the technicalities of the Sanskrit grammar in the employment of several grammatical similes. For instance, the god Brahman asks the other gods in the KS. (II, 27) whether they have been ousted from their positions by the powerful demons, just as the rules of general application (in grammar) are nullified by the following rules making exceptions. The installation of Sugrīva in place of *Vālin* is likened by Kālidāsa to the replacement of a root by its substitute in certain grammatical forms.[3]

Kālidāsa's language is faultless and free from grammatical errors and vulgarities. However, his works betray the influence of the Epics which have been definitely drawn upon by him in various ways. So the Epic influence is discernible in the vocabulary as well as in certain verbal forms employed by him. For instance, the word *go*, which is sometimes employed in the Epics[4] to denote "earth", is used in this sense by Kālidāsa in his works.[5] There is no doubt that, in comparison with the *Mahābhārata*, the *Rāmāyaṇa* has exercised much greater influence on Kālidāsa in respect of his language, style and imagery. For instance, Kālidāsa follows the *Rāmāyaṇa* in employing the word *dyo* (nominative singular *Dyauḥ*) in the feminine gender.[6] Similarly some grammatical forms such as *āsa*,[7] *tasthivāṃsam*,[8] *kāmayāna*[9] and a few forms of the periphrastic perfect with tmesis[10] found in Kālidāsa's works betray epic influence and are justifiable according to the Vedic usage, though they do not conform strictly to the rules of Pāṇinian grammar applicable to Classical Sanskrit.[11]

The language of the various characters of Kālidāsa's plays conforms to their status and situations. For instance, kings, ministers, sages, students, etc., speak Sanskrit, while women (with the exception of the nun Kauśikī), children, servants, and jesters converse in Śaurasenī but sing in Mahārāṣṭrī. The policemen and the fisherman in the Śak. speak Māgadhī. Thus the distribution of Prākrits in his plays accords with the norms fixed by the dramaturgists in this connection.[12] Kālidāsa's prose in dramatic dialogues consists of short and simple sentences.

Kālidāsa, who is noted for his metrical skill, varies the metres of his verses to suit the occasion. He generally employs long metres such as *Mandākrāntā, Śikhariṇī, Śārdūlavikrīḍita, Hariṇī, Puṣpitāgrā, Pṛthvī and Āryā* in lengthy descriptions, while short and medium metres like *Anuṣṭup, Indravajrā, Rathoddhatā, Vaṃśastha, Śālinī, Drutavilambita, Vasantatilakā* and *Mālinī* are used by him in simple narratives, normal descriptions, pithy observations and in the delineation of pathos. Kālidāsa displays his skill in the successful handling of a large number of metres exceeding twenty. Besides, he also employs a Vedic metre (*Triṣṭup*) in the Śak. (IV, 7) for the benedictory verse uttered by the sage Kaṇva to invoke the favour of the sacred Fires which Śakuntalā and others circumambulate on the occasion of bidding farewell to her.

Kālidāsa's use of imagery reveals his power of imagination, refinement of thought and aesthetic taste, his outlook on life, his keen observation of life and Nature, and his mastery of various branches of knowledge. No poet or play-wright can match Kālidāsa in the aptness and variety of similes. However, the only notable exception is Vālmīki to whom Kālidāsa is indebted for many similes. Although it is beyond the scope of the present work to determine precisely the extent of Kālidāsa's indebtedness to Vālmīki, it may be pointed out that the latter had already standardized several similes adopted by the later poets. For instance, heaven and earth, the moon and moonlight, rivers and lakes, clouds and lightning, trees and creepers, flowers (especially several varieties of the lotus) and sprouts, the pair of *Chakravāka* birds, a *Chakora*, a *Kurarī*, an elephant, a gazelle, a flamingo, etc., are already the standards of comparison in the *Rāmāyaṇa.* Kālidāsa has not only utilized such popular standards of comparison in his own ingenious and charming manner but has also invented numerous new standards of comparison to portray his miniature word-pictures. Kālidāsa's similes cover a very vast spectrum of objects ranging from the sun to a lamp and from an elephant to an insect, depending upon the nature of descriptions. The similes employed in his plays reflect the outlook and attitude of various characters towards the subjects of comparison. For instance, Duṣyanta compares his beloved Śakuntalā to a fresh flower, a rare gem, and a *Mādhavī* creeper (a spring-creeper bearing white fragrant flowers), while her foster-father Kaṇva likens her to the eastern direction and her future son to the sun; and the sage Mārīcha compares her to faith (*Śraddhā*), her son to wealth (*vitta*), and King Duṣyanta to sacred injunction (*vidhi*). Although almost all the similes employed in Kālidāsa's works are apt and praiseworthy, yet he excels in the use of those similes in which the standards of comparison are taken from Nature or everyday life, for such similes bring out his power of suggestion. A few specimens of his apt similes are given below.

King Duṣyanta describes the charm and freshness of Śakuntalā's youth and beauty by means of five different similes:[13] "I do not know the man who is destined to wed this perfect beauty who is like an unsmelt fresh flower, like a sprout unscratched by nails, like an unperforated gem, like untasted fresh honey, and like a perfect reward of meritorious deeds."

When Śakuntalā is presented by Gautamī and Kaṇva's two pupils before King Duṣyanta as his wife, he fails to recognize her due to the curse but is so much charmed by her ravishing beauty that he finds himself unable to accept or reject her as illustrated by the following simile :[14] "Pondering over the ticklish issue whether this unblemished beauty present here was previously married by me or not, I am unable to accept or repudiate her, like a bee which can neither enjoy nor give up a jasmine flower soaked in dew in the morning."

At the time of their reunion King Duṣyanta expresses his deep regret to Śakuntalā for her unjust repudiation, begs her forgiveness, and likens himself to a blind man who casts away a garland mistaking it for a snake :[15] "O fair Darling !

the rankling caused by repudiation should now disappear from your heart, because at that time my mind was under a strong delusion. People under strong delusion behave in this manner towards good things, just as a blind man casts away a garland, placed on his head, for fear of a snake."

Offering his cordial thanks to the sage Mārīcha for his miraculous favour, King Duṣyanta describes his sudden and unexpected reunion with Śakuntalā by means of two similes :[16] "A flower appears first, and then there is a fruit. Similarly rain follows the appearance of clouds. So this is the normal order of cause and effect. However, good fortunes miraculously precede your favour."

Kālidāsa employs two similes to describe Pārvatī's innate beauty exhibited by her youth :[17] "The innate beauty of her lovely form, graced with perfect and proportionate limbs, was brought out by her blooming youth, just as a painting is made life-like by the touch of a brush, and a lotus is opened up by the rays of the sun."

After snubbing the Brahmachārin, when Pārvatī started to go away, at that very moment Śiva revealed his identity and smilingly held her back (*supra*, Chapter III). Pārvatī's perplexity on this occasion is vividly described by the following simile :[18] "Having recognized him, trembling, perspiring and bearing her raised foot to step forward, perplexed Pārvatī could neither go forward nor stand there like a mountain river, the course of which has been blocked by a rock."

Kālidāsa uses three different similes from Nature to describe the beauty of Pārvatī who was being decorated with various ornaments for her wedding :[19] "Being decorated with ornaments, she looked beautiful like a creeper on which flowers are appearing, like the earlier part of night when luminaries (the moon and stars) are appearing, and like a river where birds are descending."

The condition of the kings rejected by the princess Indumatī at her *Svayaṃvara* is aptly described by the poet through the following simile :[20] "As soon as Indumatī, who was to choose a husband for herself, passed by any of the assembled kings (rejecting him), he became pallid like a highway turret which has been left behind by a moving lamp-flame at night." The use of *Dīpa-śikhā* (lamp-flame) in this simile has earned him the epithet of *Dīpaśikhā-Kālidāsa.*

Through another simile of the flame of a lamp Kālidāsa describes, as follows, the collapse of King Aja with his wife Indumatī :[21] "When Indumatī was collapsing, she brought down her husband to the ground with her lifeless body; for, a particle of the flame of an oil-lamp falls on the ground with a drop of oil."

The simile of an oil-lamp is again employed by Kālidāsa to describe Daśaratha's old age :[22] "He, who had amply enjoyed the pleasures of life, reached old age and was about to attain final emancipation like the flame of an oil-lamp which, after consuming entire oil and reaching the end of the wick, is about to go out in the morning." In this verse the poet uses *double entendre.*

In the Māl. when King Agnimitra sees his beloved Mālavikā clad in new garments and decorated with ornaments, he describes her beauty with the following simile of a star-lit night :[23] "Mālavikā, who has put on fit silken garments and who is adorned with numerous ornaments, looks beautiful like vernal night (literally : the night of the month of *Chaitra)* which is resplendent with stars fully visible in the clear sky free from frost, and in which the moonlight is about to appear."

In the Vik. when King Purūravas sees Urvaśī flying to heaven with her friends, he describes the state of his mind with the following simile :[24] "Flying in the sky, this nymph forcibly tears away my mind from my body, just as a goose tears a fibre from the broken tip of the root of a lotus."

In the *Ṛtusaṃhāra* the poet likens the earth, which is red with the blossoming *Kiṃśuka* trees, to a new bride clad in a red garment :[25] "In Spring the earth, which is covered with the *Kiṃśuka* trees laden with red flowers shaken by winds and resembling burning fires, looks charming like a new bride clad in a red raiment."

In the Megh. the exiled Yakṣa, who begs a cloud to convey his message to his separated wife, gives the following figurative description of his native city Alakā which is compared to a lovely maiden :[26] "O free wanderer ! you will not fail to recognize at first sight Alakā which, situated on the higher level of Mount Kailāsa with the river Gaṅgā flowing nearby at a lower level, looks like a lovely maiden in her lover's lap with her white silken garment slipping down; and which, having lofty mansions with raining clouds hovering over them, looks in the rainy season like a cheerful lovely maiden whose tresses are decorated with strings of pearls." *Double entendre* is used by the poet in this verse.

In the Ragh., which is considered to be a work of his mature age, Kālidāsa exhibits his vast learning by choosing the standards of comparison in his similes not only from Nature and everyday life but also from grammar, medicine, astronomy, *Arthaśāstra*, religious rites, and philosophy. Unless and until a reader is familiar with the technicalities of all these branches of knowledge, he finds it difficult to appreciate fully the aptness of such similes. Barring a few similes of this type, Kālidāsa's similes are, on the whole, so apt and suggestive that an average reader can easily enjoy and appreciate their poetic excellence.

In addition to various types of similes, several other figures of speech based on comparison are aptly employed in Kālidāsa's works. Among such figures of speech metaphor (*rūpaka*), poetic fancy (*utprekṣā*), exemplification (*dṛṣṭānta*), illustration (*nidarśanā*), corroboration (*arthāntaranyāsa*) and hyperbole (*atiśayokti*) are particularly noteworthy.

It is important to note here that Kālidāsa's well-known sayings, which are embodied in the figure of speech styled as *Arthāntaranyāsa* (corroboration), afford us an insight into his sagacity, culture and keen observation. A few selected examples of his famous apothegms are cited below.

Kālidāsa coins a pithy saying about the large-heartedness of great men in the context of describing the Himālaya mountain personified as a divine being :[27] "The Himālaya mountain protects from the sun during day-time darkness, hidden in his caves out of fear, as it were; for, *great persons protect even a mean fellow like their own good man, when he has taken refuge with them.*"

The perseverance of a resolute man to pursue his aim in the face of temptation is illustrated by Śiva's permission to Pārvatī to serve him during the period of his meditation :[28] "Siva permitted Pārvatī to serve him, even though she was an impediment to his meditation; for, *only those persons are really resolute whose minds remain unaffected even in the face of temptation.*"

The maxim that one's own creation should not be destroyed under any circumstances is expressed by Kālidāsa in the following words of Brahman (Creator) who was requested by the gods to destroy the demon Tāraka :[9] "It is not proper for me to exterminate the demon who owes his prosperity to me ; for, *one should not cut down even a poisonous tree, after it has been reared.*"

In the description of Pārvatī's strong determination to pursue her aim, the poet employs an *Arthāntaranyāsa* figure of speech, expressing an apt apothegm :[30] "In spite of her best efforts, Menā could not dissuade her daughter Pārvatī from undertaking severe austerities. *Who can turn a determined mind away from its desired object, or who can reverse the downward flow of gushing waters ?*"

The saying that a gem which is sought after by everybody need not run after people is contained in the following figure of speech employed by Kālidāsa to describe Pārvatī's position in the eyes of Śiva who disguised as a Brahmachārin asks her the purpose of her austerities :[31] "If you seek to attain heaven through these austerities, your effort is futile, because the regions of your father (i.e. the Himalayan regions) form part of heaven. And if you desire to obtain a husband, you need not bother at all; for, *a gem does not run after people, but it is sought after by them.*"

The maxim that virtue is esteemed everywhere without any consideration of sex or age is expressed by the poet in the description of Arundhatī who along with the Seven Seers came to see Śiva :[32] "Siva looked upon Arundhatī and the Seers with equal regard ; for, *the consideration of sex is irrelevant and only the good conduct of virtuous people is adored.*"

Kālidāsa's popular saying about the contribution of good wives to the performance of religious acts is contained in the following stanza :[33] "After his meeting with Arundhatī, Śiva's regard for wives increased further ; for, *good wives are mainly instrumental in the performance of religious rites.*"

To corroborate their suggestion to Himālaya about Pārvatī's marriage with Śiva, the Seven Seers employ the following figurative expression :[34] "It would be proper for you to unite your daughter in wedlock with Śiva, just as speech is united with appropriate meaning ; for, *a daughter married to a good husband brings about no worry to her father*."

Himālaya's gesture in seeking his wife's concurrence for promising Pārvatī's hand to Śiva in response to the abovementioned suggestion of the Seven Seers is justified by the poet through an apothegm :[35] "Although the proposal made by the Seven Seers about Pārvatī's marriage with Śiva had fulfilled Himālaya's long-cherished desire, yet he significantly looked at Menā's face to seek her concurrence; for, *householders are generally guided by their wives in matters concerning their daughters*."

Another apothegm is coined by Kālidāsa to support Menā's instant approval of her husband's proposal :[36] "Menā also accepted her husband's desired proposal, because *devoted wives never act contrary to the desire of their husbands*."

Raghu's munificence following his all-round conquests is justified by the poet through a maxim :[37] "After his conquest in all quarters Raghu performed the *Viśvajit* sacrifice at which he gave away his entire wealth in charity; for, *virtuous people receive a thing with a view to gifting it away, just as clouds receive water from the earth in order to rain it*."

The futility of efforts to revive Aja's wife Indumatī is figuratively described in the following stanza :[38] "Although King Aja regained consciousness after he was given some such treatment as fanning, she remained lifeless as before; for, *treatment can succeed in the case of that person only who is destined to live for some time more*."

Kālidāsa's following saying to justify Duṣyanta's love for Śakuntalā at first sight without knowing anything about her is very popular among the students of Sanskrit literature :[39] "She should undoubtedly be eligible to be the consort of a Kṣatriya for the simple reason that my noble mind longs for her; for, *virtuous persons' dictate of conscience is their final authority in matters of doubt*."

The old saying that love-sick people are unable to discriminate between animate and inanimate objects is cited by Kālidāsa in the Megh. to justify the Yakṣa's request to a cloud to convey his message to his wife :[40] "There can be no connection whatsoever between a cloud which consists of only smoke, light, water and wind, and a meaningful message which can be conveyed through only sentient beings possessed of proficient faculties of senses. However, completely ignoring this fact, the Yakṣa in his eagerness requested the cloud to convey his message; *for, love-sick people are unable to discriminate between sentient and insentient beings.*"

The Yakṣa justifies his request to the cloud by an apothegm :[41] "I know that you are Indra's important functionary capable of assuming any form at will, and you belong to the world-renowned family of the best clouds. This is why I approach you with a request on account of my misfortune of being far away from my wife; for, *a request rejected by a virtuous person is better than the one granted by a mean fellow.*"

An important maxim is coined by Kālidāsa in the following stanza containing the Yakṣa's advice to the Cloud Messenger in its northward journey :[42] "When you have depleted your water, you should proceed further only after replenishing yourself with the *Revā's* water, which has been scented by the fragrant rut of forest elephants, and the flow of which has been obstructed by the groves of *Jambū* trees. O Cloud ! when you possess internal essence, the wind will not be able to toss you up in the sky ; for, *everything empty is light, while fullness leads to heaviness* (*as well as greatness*)."

A saying pertaining to the disposition of tender-hearted people is contained in the following stanza of the Megh. in which the Yakṣa describes the pathetic condition of his separated wife to the Cloud Messenger :[43] "The pathetic condition of the helpless lady, whom you will find devoid of ornaments and tossing her frail body to and fro in great agony on his bed, will undoubtedly move you to tears in the form of fresh showers ; for, *tender-hearted people are generally disposed to pity a person in distress.*"

Notes and References

1. Daṇḍin in his *Kāvyādarśa* (I, 41-42) calls it the *Vaidarbha mārga* and enumerates its following ten qualities :—

   श्लेषः प्रसादः समता माधुर्यं सुकुमारता ।

   अर्थव्यक्तिरुदारत्वमोजः कान्तिसमाधयः ॥

   इति वैदर्भमार्गस्य प्राणा दश गुणाः स्मृताः ।

   However, the later rhetoricians name it *Vaidarbhī rīti*; cf. *Sāhitya-darpaṇa* (IX, 2-3) :

   माधुर्यव्यजकैर्वर्णै रचना ललितात्मिका । अवृत्तिरल्पवृत्तिर्वा वैदर्भी रीतिरिष्यते ॥

2. Ragh. II, 53 : *kṣatra*; III, 21 : *Raghu*; IV, 12 : *rājan* (cf. R. II, 3,44); X, 67 : *Rāma*; KS. I, 26 : *Umā*; V, 28 : *Aparṇā*.
3. Ragh. XII, 58; cf., e.g., the replacement of the root √*as* "to be" by *bhū* (Pāṇini II, 4, 52), and that of √*brū* by *vach* (Pāṇini II, 4, 53).
4. Cf. R. I, 48, 4; II, 29, 23; Mbh. I, 58, 6; III, 33, 18; 158, 13; etc.
5. *See*, e.g., Ragh. I, 26; V, 2; X, 72; XI, 36; KS. VI, 68. But in the Ragh. V, 12, etc., the word *go* is used by Kālidāsa to denote "speech" also.
6. *See*, e.g., Ragh. V, 33; R. I, 114, 13; IV, 28, 3; cf. R. II, 114, 13; IV, 28, 3. In the early Vedic language the word *dyo* is mostly used in the masculine gender, but the tendency of its feminine use is met with in some Vedic passages; cf. our *Vaidika Vyākaraṇa*, Vol. I, p. 242.
7. KS. I, 35—perfect of √*as* "to be" which ought to be *babhūva* in Classical Sanskrit (see Note 3 above), but is permissible in the Vedic language; cf. our *Vaidika Vyākaraṇa*, Vol. II, pp. 534ff.
8. Ragh. V, 61—perfect participle of √*sthā*. According to Pāṇini (III, 2, 108), this formation is not allowed in Classical Sanskrit, but it is quite common in the Vedic language; cf. *Vaidika Vyākaraṇa*, Vol. II, p. 759; see Ragh. IX, 59—*Uttasthuṣaḥ*; X, 77—*petuṣī*. KS. VI, 72—*āsthuṣā*. Such forms are met with in the R. and the Mbh.
9. Ragh. XIX, 50—the present participle of √kam in violation of Pāṇini III, 1, 35 (*kāmayamāna*). But such forms occur in the Epics; cf. *chintayāna* in the Mbh. I, 229, 8; III, 41, 5; etc.
10. Ragh. IX, 61—

    तं पातयां प्रथममास पपात पश्चात् ;

    XIII, 36—

    प्रभंशयां यो नहुषं चकार ;

    XVI, 86—

    संयोजयां विधिवदास ;

    cf. *Vaidika Vyākaraṇa*, Vol. II, pp. 543-44.
11. Attempts made by the later grammarians and commentators to justify

such grammatical forms in accordance with the usage of Classical Sanskrit are futile; cf. Mallinātha's commentary on KS. I, 35. Some scholars regard grammatical forms of this type as examples of Vedicism (cf. Pratap Bandopādhyāya : *Vedicism in Kālidāsa*, Proceedings of All-India Oriental Conference, 23rd Session, pp. 300 ff.). But in my opinion Kālidāsa has used such non-Pāṇinian grammatical forms under the influence of the Epics rather than the Vedic literature direct, though he is an ardent champion of Vedic thought and culture as discussed by us elsewhere; for he is more indebted to the Epics than to the Vedic literature for his ideas and expression.

12. Cf. Sāhitya-darpaṇa, VI, 158-169.

13. अनाघ्रातं पुष्पं किसलयमलूनं कररुहै—
रनाविद्धं रत्नं मधु नवमनास्वादितरसम् ।
अखण्डं पुण्यानां फलमिव च तद्रूपमनघं
न जाने भोक्तारं कमिह समुपस्थास्यति विधिः ॥
(Śak., II, 10)

14. इदमुपनतमेवं रूपमक्लिष्टकान्ति
प्रथमपरिगृहीतं स्यान्न वेति व्यवस्यन् ।
भ्रमर इव विभाते कुन्दमन्तस्तुषारं
न च खलु परिभोक्तुं नैव शक्नोमि हातुम् ॥
(Śak., V. 19)

15. सुतनु ! हृदयात्प्रत्यादेशव्यलीकमपैतु ते
किमपि मनसः संमोहो मे तदा बलवानभूत् ।
प्रबलतमसामेवंप्रायाः शुभेषु प्रवृत्तयः
स्रजमपि शिरस्यन्धः क्षिप्तां धुनोत्यहिशंकया ॥
(Śak., VII, 24)

16. उदेति पूर्वं कुसुमं ततः फलं
घनोदयः प्राक् तदनन्तरं पयः ।
निमित्तनैमित्तिकयोरयं क्रम—
स्तव प्रसादस्य पुरस्तु संपदः ॥
(Śak., VII, 30)

These two similes are employed in the KS. (VI, 54) also when Pārvatī's father Himālaya welcomes the Seven Seers on their arrival in his Capital on behalf of Śiva.

17. उन्मीलितं तूलिकयेव चित्रं
सूर्यांशुभिर्भिन्नमिवारविन्दम् ।
बभूव तस्याश्चतुरस्रशोभि
वपुर्विभक्तं नवयौवनेन ॥
(KS. I, 32)

18. तं वीक्ष्य वेपथुमती सरसांगयष्टि—
निक्षेपणाय पदमुद्धृतमुद्वहन्ती ।
मार्गाचलव्यतिकराकुलितेव सिन्धुः
शैलाधिराजतनया न ययौ न तस्थौ ॥

(KS. V, 85)

19. सा संभवद्भिः कुसुमैर्लतेव ज्योतिर्भिरुद्यद्भिरिव त्रियामा ।
सरिद् विहंगैरिव लीयमानैरामुच्यमानाभरणा चकासे ॥

(KS. VII, 21)

20. संचारिणी दीपशिखेव रात्रौ यं यं व्यतीयाय पतिवरा सा ।
नरेन्द्रमार्गाट्ट इव प्रपेदे विवर्णभावं स स भूमिपालः ॥

(Ragh. VI, 67)

21. वपुषा करणोज्झितेन सा निपतन्ती पतिमप्यपातयत् ।
ननु तैलनिषेकबिन्दुना सह दीपार्चिरुपैति मेदिनीम् ॥

(Ragh. VIII, 38)

22. निर्विष्टविषयस्नेहः स दशान्तमुपेयिवान् ।
आसीदासन्ननिर्वाणः प्रदीपार्चिरिवोषसि ॥

(Ragh. XII, 1)

23. अनतिलम्बिदुकूलनिवासिनी बहुभिराभरणैः प्रतिभाति मे ।
उडुगणैरुदयोन्मुखचन्द्रिका हतहिमैरिव चैत्रविभावरी ॥

(Māl. V, 7)

24. एषा मनो मे प्रसभं शरीरात्पितुः पदं मध्यममुत्पतन्ती ।
सुरांगना कर्षति खण्डिताग्रात्सूत्रं मृणालादिव राजहंसी ॥

(Vik. I, 20)

25. आदीप्तवह्निसदृशैर्मरुतावधूतैः
सर्वत्र किंशुकवनैः कुसुमावनम्रैः ।
सद्यो वसन्तसमये हि समाचितेयं
रक्तांशुका नववधूरिव भाति भूमिः ।

(RS. VI, 19)

26. तस्योत्संगे प्रणयिन इव स्रस्तगंगादुकूलां
न त्वं दृष्ट्वा न पुनरलकां ज्ञास्यसे कामचारिन् ।
या वः काले वहति सलिलोद्गारमुच्चैर्विमाना
मुक्ताजालग्रथितमलकं कामिनीवाभ्रवृन्दम् ॥

(Pūrvamegha, 63)

27. दिवाकराद्रक्षति यो गुहासु लीनं दिवा भीतमिवान्धकारम् ।
क्षुद्रेऽपि नूनं शरणं प्रपन्ने ममत्वमुच्चैःशिरसां सतीव ॥

(KS. I, 12)

28. प्रत्यर्थिभूतामपि तां समाधेः शुश्रूषमाणां गिरिशोऽनुमेने ।
विकारहेतौ सति विक्रियन्ते येषां न चेतांसि त एव धीराः ॥
(KS. I, 59)

29. इतः स दैत्यः प्राप्तश्रीर्नेत एवार्हति क्षयम् ।
विषवृक्षोऽपि संवर्ध्य स्वयं छेत्तुमसांप्रतम् ॥
(KS. II, 55)

30. इति ध्रुवेच्छामनुशासती सुतां शशाक मेना न नियन्तुमुद्यमात् ।
क ईप्सितार्थस्थिरनिश्चयं मनः पयश्च निम्नाभिमुखं प्रतीपयेत् ॥
(KS. V, 5)

31. दिवं यदि प्रार्थयसे वृथा श्रमः पितुः प्रदेशास्तव देवभूमयः ।
अथोपयन्तारमलं समाधिना न रत्नमन्विष्यति मृग्यते हि तत् ॥
(KS. V, 45)

A similar idea is expressed in the Śak. III, 11, cd :
लभेत वा प्रार्थयिता न वा श्रियं
श्रिया दुरापः कथमीप्सितो भवेत् ।

32. तामगौरवभेदेन मुनींश्चापश्यदीश्वरः ।
स्त्री पुमानित्यनास्थैषा वृत्तं हि महितं सताम् ॥
(KS. VI, 12)

Cf. Bhavabhūti's view :—
गुणाः पूजास्थानं गुणिषु न च लिंगं न च वयः ।
(Uttararāmacharita IV, 11)

33. तद्दर्शनादभूच्छंभोर्भूयान्दारार्थमादरः ।
क्रियाणां खलु धर्म्याणां सत्पत्न्यो मूलकारणम् ॥
(KS. VI, 13)

34. तमर्थमिव भारत्या सुतया योक्तुमर्हसि ।
अशोच्या हि पितुः कन्या सद्भर्तृप्रतिपादिता ॥
(KS. VI, 79)

35. शैलः संपूर्णकामोऽपि मेनामुखमुदैक्षत ।
प्रायेण गृहिणीनेत्राः कन्यार्थेषु कुटुम्बिनः ॥
(KS. VI, 85)

36. मेने मेनापि तत्सर्वं पत्युः कार्यमभीप्सितम् ।
भवन्त्यव्यभिचारिण्यो भर्तुरिष्टे पतिव्रताः ॥
(KS. VI, 86)

37. स विश्वजितमाजह्रे यज्ञं सर्वस्वदक्षिणम् ।
आदानं हि विसर्गाय सतां वारिमुचामिव ॥
(Ragh. IV, 86)

38. नृपतेर्व्यंजनादिभिस्तमो नुनुदे सा तु तथैव संस्थिता ।
प्रतिकारविधानमायुष: सति शेषे हि फलाय कल्पते ॥
(Ragh. VIII, 40)

39. असंशयं क्षत्रपरिग्रहक्षमा यदार्यमस्यामभिलाषि मे मनः ।
सतां हि संदेहपदेषु वस्तुषु प्रमाणमन्तःकरणप्रवृत्तयः ॥
(Śak. I, 19)

40. धूमज्योतिःसलिलमरुतां संनिपातः क्व मेघः
संदेशार्थाः क्व पटुकरणैः प्राणिभिः प्रापणीयाः ।
इत्यौत्सुक्यादपरिगणयन्गुह्यकस्तं ययाचे
कामार्ता हि प्रकृतिकृपणाश्चेतनाचेतनेषु ॥
(Pūrvamegha, 5)

41. जातं वंशे भुवनविदिते पुष्करावर्तकानां
जानामि त्वां प्रकृतिपुरुषं कामरूपं मघोनः ।
तेनार्थित्वं त्वयि विधिवशाद्दूरबन्धुर्गतोऽहं
याच्ञा मोघा वरमधिगुणे नाधमे लब्धकामा ॥
(Pūrvamegha, 6)

42. तस्यास्तिक्तैर्वनगजमदैर्वासितं वान्तवृष्टि—
र्जम्बूकुंजप्रतिहतरयं तोयमादाय गच्छेः ।
अन्तःसारं घन ! तुलयितुं नानिलः शक्ष्यति त्वां
रिक्तः सर्वो भवति हि लघुः पूर्णता गौरवाय ।
(Pūrvamegha, 20)

Mallinātha reads a medical meaning also into this stanza.

43. सा संन्यस्ताभरणमबला पेशलं धारयन्ती
शय्योत्संगे निहितमसकृद् दुःखदुःखेन गात्रम् ।
त्वामप्यस्रं नवजलमयं मोचयिष्यत्यवश्यं
प्रायः सर्वो भवति करुणावृत्तिरार्द्रान्तरात्मा ॥
(Uttaramegha, 30)

6

Kālidāsa's Treatment of Nature

Kālidāsa whose poetic genius is inspired by Nature excels in the description of natural scenery in its beautiful, charming and sympathetic aspects. It is no exaggeration to say that the excellent and elevating description of Nature is the very soul of Kālidāsa's poetry. The *Ṛtusamhāra*, which is regarded as his youthful production, is solely devoted to the description of Nature in different seasons as viewed by a lover. His other lyric poem, *Meghadūta*, presents a more mature description of Nature from the viewpoint of a separated lover. The epic poem *Kumārasambhava* hinges on the description of the mountain Himālaya. The plot of his masterpiece, *Abhijñāna-Śākuntala*, is mainly set in the natural surroundings of the hermitages of the sages Kaṇva and Mārīcha. Kālidāsa's other three works, viz., the *Raghuvaṃśa*, the *Vikramorvaśīya* and the *Mālavikāgnimitra*, are also characterized by the description of Nature in varying degrees.

The description of Nature is inseparable from Kālidāsa's poetry, just as the moonlight is inseparable from the moon. He displays not only his great power of imagination and keen observation but also the refinement of his aesthetic taste and his concept of beauty in the description of Nature. For instance, the poet through his extraordinary power of imagination presents in the Ragh. an imaginative description of the natural scenery of India as viewed by Rāma and his companions in the course of their journey from Lankā to Ayodhyā in the aerial car called *Puṣpaka*. The poet imagines that the ocean, as seen from the aerial car, resembles an iron wheel ; and that the beach appearing blue with the rows of *Tamāla* and *Tālī* (a kind of palm tree) trees looks from afar like a thin streak of rusty spots on the edge of the iron wheel.[1] The calm and clear current of a river named *Mandākinī* in the vicinity of Mount Chitrakūṭa appears thin from the sky like a necklace of pearls around the neck of the earth.[2] Presenting an aerial view of the confluence of the rivers Gaṅgā and Yamunā, Kālidāsa imagines that the former mingled in its flow with the waves of the latter looks at one place like a necklace of pearls inlaid with sapphires emitting lustre, at another place like a garland of white lotus flowers interwoven with blue lotuses, and somewhere else like a flock of white swans intermingled with geese called *Kādamba* having dark-grey wings.[3] Similarly an imaginary description of the landscape, as surveyed from the sky, is contained in Act VII of the Śak. When King Duṣyanta is descending from the heaven to the earth in the celestial aerial car driven by Mātali, the scene below is described by the former to the latter as follows :[4] "The earth appears to descend from the peaks of the emerging mountains; with the emergence of their trunks the trees seem to withdraw from hiding under their own foliage; and the rivers, which previously appeared to be waterless due to their indistinctness from high altitude, present themselves now in full view with their expanse. See the wonder : it looks as if the earth is being brought near me by someone who is throwing it up."

Kālidāsa's keen observation of Nature is revealed in his description of seasons, mountains, forests, rivers, lakes, trees, plants, creepers, flowers, animals, birds and insects. In the *Ṛtusamhāra* the poet describes the plight of thirsty deer in Summer as follows :[5] "The mouths of the deer parched by the fierce heat of the sun have become dry due to intense thirst, and they run about in the forest, mistaking the illusory collyrium-like sky for water." Another verse of the RS. contains an equally vivid description of birds and animals afflicted with excessive heat in Summer :[6] "Birds perched on leafless trees are panting ; fatigued monkeys resort to a mountain bower ; Gayals roam about in search of water ; and *Śarabhas* lift up water from a well to drink." Kālidāsa vividly describes flowing rain-water :[7] "Fresh and muddy rain-water, mixed with insects, dust and blades of grass, moves in a zig-zag course like a snake, and flows down, while frightened frogs cautiously look at it."

In the Śak. there is a picturesque description of the deer who, being pursued by King Duṣyanta, runs for his life :[8] "Bending his neck gracefully, the deer glances time and again at the chasing chariot ; fearing the fall of an arrow, he closely draws the hinder part of his body into the front part ; his path is strewn with half-chewed blades of Darbha grass dropped from his mouth opened in fatigue; due to his high leaps he runs more in the air than on the ground."

The description of natural scenery belonging to the whole country displays Kālidāsa's broad vision, national outlook and minute observation. For instance, in Canto IV of the Ragh. he describes the vineries of Persia ; the walnut trees of the *Kamboja* country ; the saffron plant growing on the banks of the river Indus (or the Oxus, *see* Note 12 of Chapter II) ; the sandal forests infested with snakes on the southern mountains *Malaya* and *Dardura* ; the groves of pepper plants in the valleys of the mount *Malaya* ; the pearl-fishery in the Bay of Bengal adjacent to the mouth of the river *Tāmraparṇī* ; the cardamom plant and the trees named *Ketaka*, *Puṃnāga* (*Nāgakeśara*) and *Rājatālī* growing in the South ; the forests of palm trees on the eastern coast ; a variety of rice known as *Kalama* cultivated in the eastern part of India ; the betel-plant growing in Orissa ; the rows of fruit-laden betel-nut trees on the eastern coast ; the herbs, musk-deer, minerals, bamboos, birch-trees, *Sarala* trees, and *deodar* trees of the Himalayas ; and the black aloe trees of *Prāgjyotiṣa* (*supra*, Note 15 of Chapter III). Kālidāsa, who seems to be very fond of mountains, misses no opportunity to describe them. A very beautiful and charming description of the Himalayas is contained in the KS. which describes the snow-clad mountain range as the treasure-house of innumerable precious stones, minerals, important herbs, trees, plants and creepers with delightful flowers ; as the abode of the *Siddhas*, ascetics, *Yakṣas*, *Kinnaras*, *Kirātas* and various types of animals and birds ; as the source of the Gaṅgā and several other rivers ; and as possessed of lofty peaks and dark caves. Kālidāsa's lyrical poem *Meghadūta* portrays a very fascinating picture of the Himalayas where the exiled Yakṣa's native city *Alakā*, governed by the god Kubera, is situated. Mapping the path of the Cloud-Messenger to Alakā, the Yakṣa describes the Himalayan scenery right from *Kanakhala*, where the river Gaṅgā enters the plains, up to Alakā : the crystal clear waters of the river Gaṅgā, snowy peaks of the mountain scented with the smell of musk deer, forests teeming with various animals such as the Yak and the *Śarabha*, resounding bamboo-trees, echoing caves, the white peaks of the Kailāsa serving as the mirror of the gods' wives, the lake Mānasa abounding in golden lotuses, and the enchanting scenic beauty of Alakā. The poet attempts in his epic poem Ragh. (IV, 71-84) a very brief description of the Himalayas from Kashmir to Kāmarūpa, mentioning the lofty peaks, minerals, caves, several trees such as the birch, the bamboo, the *Nameru*, the *Sarala*, the deodar and the black Aloe, several animals such as the lion, the elephant and the musk deer, the rivers *Gaṅgā* and *Lauhityā* (Brahmaputra), the *Kinnaras*, the *Kirātas* and other hill tribes. The forest of the *Gandhamādana* mountain on the Himalayas is described in Act IV of the Vik. King Purūravas, who madly roams about in the forest in search of his beloved Urvaśī, addresses the mountain peaks, clouds, streams, trees, creepers, animals, birds and insects (*supra*, Chapter IV). A very beautiful description of Nature is contained in the stanzas uttered by Purūravas. A very fascinating description of the *Gandhamādana* forest is contained in the KS.[9] In the last Act of the Śak. Kālidāsa describes the natural scenery of the mountain Hemakūṭa[10] of the *Kiṃpuruṣa* country where the hermitage of the sage Mārīcha is situated (*supra*, Chapter IV).

In the first half of the Megh. Kālidāsa describes the natural scenery of the Vindhya mountain, its rivers and a number of hills (*supra*, Chapter III) in the rainy season. The Vindhyas are depicted as abounding in numerous ornamental trees, plants and creepers such as the yellowish-brown *Kadamba*, the *Kuṭaja*, the *Ketaka*, the *Kadalī* (a plant with white flowers) and the *Yūthikā* (a kind of jasmine), which all blossom in the rainy season, the *Jambū* tree which is laden with black fruits at this time, and the *Udumbara* (a kind of fig-tree) which bears fruits in this season. From among the animals, birds and insects of the Vindhya region the elephant, the spotted deer (*Sāraṅga*), the peacock, the crane, (*Sārasa*), the *Chātaka*, and the bee are particularly chosen for description by the poet in the Megh.

We have already (*supra*, Chapter III) spoken of the rivers of the Vindhya range. In the RS. also Kālidāsa describes the natural scenery of the Vindhyas in the rainy season. The poet imagines that the clouds, bent down with water contained in them, seem to gladden with showers the Vindhya mountain scorched by the excessive heat of Summer, deeming it to be their lofty resort.[11] Describing the sylvan beauty of the mountain in the rainy season, the poet says that the Vindhya forests, looking attractive due to the sprouting trees and the tender shoots of green grass mauled by deer, delight our mind.[12] In the Māl. King Agnimitra likens himself to the Vindhya mountain and his angry and weeping Queen Irāvatī, who is about to strike him with her golden girdle, to a row of raining clouds, which strikes the mountain with lightning.[13] In the Ragh. Rāma, who did not violate the rules of righteous conduct during his stay at *Pañchavaṭī*, is compared by the poet to the Vindhya mountain which is believed to stay in its original form without growing in height.[14] Moreover, Rāma, who is sprinkled with waters collected from various seas, rivers and lakes for his royal consecration, is compared by Kālidāsa to the Vindhya mountain being showered with rain waters.[15] The mount *Chitrakūṭa*, resounding with the sound of waterfalls and having clouds on its peaks, is likened to a bellowing wild bull whose horns are covered with mud in sportive butting.[16] Describing the natural scenery of the mountains in the rainy season, the poet (RS. II, 16) says that the mountains, being kissed by lotus-like white clouds, and abounding in waterfalls and dancing peacocks, delight our hearts.

The Ragh. contains a vivid description of the Indian Ocean and its beach. Whales, which swallow in their wide-open mouths aquatic creatures with water at the mouth of rivers, discharge jets of water from their perforative heads by closing their jaws.[17] When the sea foams, which are ripped into two by the sudden emergence of elephant-like crocodiles, reach their cheeks, they (the sea-foams) look for a moment like their ear-chowries.[18] The sea snakes, which emerge from water to breathe in fresh air at the beach and which are hardly distinguishable from the rolling waves, can be spotted by means of the shining gems of their hoods in the sunlight.[19] A cluster of conch-shells suddenly thrown up by strong waves on coral reefs drift away somehow with great difficulty, as their apertures are entangled in the erect shoots of the coral reefs.[20] The poet imagines that the ocean with a cloud revolving over it due to a whirlpool appears as if it (the ocean) is again being churned by means of a mountain.[21] The sands of the sea-coast are strewn with a mass of pearls issued from open oyster shells thrown ashore by waves, and there are rows of betel-nut trees laden with fruits along the sea-coast.[22] Kālidāsa metaphorically describes the earth as a cow and the ocean as her udder.[23]

Several rivers of the North and the South are described in the works of Kālidāsa. In the RS. there is a general description of rivers in various seasons. Washing away trees grown on their banks with their strong currents of muddy water, the rivers in the rainy season flow fast to the ocean in a flurry like corrupt women.[24] In Autumn the rivers flow slowly like young, beautiful and intoxicated ladies, having golden girdles in the form of moving glittering fish and pearl-necklaces in the form of rows of white birds perched on their banks.[25] The river Gaṅgā is described by Kālidāsa in various contexts. In the KS. Umā' s quick attainment of learning, already acquired by her in her previous birth, is compared to the arrival of flamingoes on the banks of the Gaṅgā in Autumn ;[26] and Śiva's favourite Himalayan peak full of *deodar* trees watered by the streams of the Gaṅgā is spoken of in another verse of the same epic.[27] *Oṣadhiprastha*, the capital of Umā's father Himālaya, is described in the KS. as surrounded by the waters of the river Gaṅgā like a moat.[28] In the Megh. the poet first describes the Gaṅgā near *Kanakhala* where it descends from the Himalayas and enters the plains.[29] Kālidāsa imagines that, if the Cloud-Messenger bends down obliquely to drink the crystal clear water of the Gaṅgā, the shadow of the dark cloud falling on the stream would create there a delightful artificial spectacle of the confluence of the Gaṅgā and the Yamunā.[30] As already pointed out above (Note 26 of Chapter V), the Gaṅgā flowing by Alakā on Mount Kailāsa is likened by the poet to a white silken garment.[31] In another verse of this lyric poem the poet imaginatively describes the heavenly maidens, wooed by the gods, as playing with gems to be searched after concealment in the golden sands on the banks of the river *Mandākinī* (*Gaṅgā*), in its cool breeze under the shade of coral trees.[32] In the Ragh. Kālidāsa describes the Gaṅgā in various similes, besides giving its aerial description (*see* Note 3). Raghu, leading his great army to the eastern ocean in the course of his *Digvijaya*, is compared to Bhagīratha taking the river Gaṅgā, fallen from Śiva's matted hair, to the eastern ocean.[33] The poet likens the various philosophical systems for attaining final emancipation to the divergent branches of the Gaṅgā near its mouth.[34] Slender-waisted Kausalyā, sleeping by the side of infant Rāma, looked graceful like the thin stream of the Gaṅgā with the offering of lotuses on its sands in Autumn.[35] The river Sarayū, on the banks of which the ancient city of Ayodhyā was situated, is vividly described in the Ragh., and the confluence of the Gaṅgā and the Sarayū is regarded as sacred as that of the Gaṅgā and the Yamunā. On his return journey from Laṅka to Ayodhyā in the aerial car called Puṣpaka, Rāma tells Sītā that the sages declare the lake Mānasa, abounding in golden lotuses enjoyed by heavenly maidens, to be the source of the river Sarayū whose waters, sanctified by the final bath of the Ikṣvākus at the performance of their Aśvamedha sacrifices, flow to the capital city of Ayodhyā ; which (Sarayū) is esteemed by him as the common foster-mother of the *Uttara-Kosalas* for rearing them in her lap in the form of the sands of her banks, with her abundant milk in the form of her waters ; and which (Sarayū), separated like Rāma's mother from his revered father (King Daśaratha), embraces Rāma on his return from exile with her arms in the form of her waves accompanied by the cool breeze.[36] King Kuśa's water-sport with the ladies of his harem in the river Sarayū is graphically described by the poet in the Ragh.[37] The river Śiprā, on the bank of which the city of Ujjayinī is situated, is fondly described by the poet. In the Ragh. Kālidāsa mentions the pleasure-gardens refreshed by the cool breeze passing through the waves of the river Śiprā.[38] It is said in the Megh. that the Śiprā's pleasant morning breeze, which is fragrant with the perfume of blooming lotuses and which prolongs the eloquent, low and sweet cooing of cranes, relieves the amoristic languor of ladies like a lover adept in wooing.[39] The river Narmadā (*alias* Revā), flowing in several streams at the foot of the Vindhya mountain through its rugged rocks, looks like a decorative painting in divergent lines of colour on the body of an elephant.[40] There is a very beautiful and imaginative description of the river *Charmaṇvatī* (modern Chambal) in the Megh. The Yakṣa tells the Cloud Messenger that when the Cloud, which appears dark by stealing the complexion of Lord Kṛṣṇa, bends down to drink water from the river's broad stream looking thin from a distance, the celestial beings will witness this spectacular sight : as if it (the river) is a necklace of a single string of pearls, studded with a large sapphire in the centre, around the neck of the earth.[41]

Kālidāsa often describes in his works the natural scenery of lakes adorned with trees, creepers, flowers, fish and birds. In Autumn the lakes, which are adorned with the pairs of merry flamingoes and blooming white and blue lotuses, and in which rows of waves are stirred by the mild morning breeze, delight our hearts.[42] In Winter also the lakes, having clear and cold water, and adorned with blue lotuses and gay geese, fascinate the minds of people.[43] The lake *Mānasa* (alias *Mānasarovara, Brahmasaras*) is often described by the poet as full of golden lotuses, inhabited by flamingoes, and possessed of crystal clear water.[44] Kālidāsa briefly refers to the natural beauty of the lake *Pampā* vividly described in the Rāmāyaṇa.[45]

Trees, plants, creepers, flowers, birds and animals which figure prominently in Kālidāsa's description of seasons, mountains, forests, rivers, lakes and sea-shores form an important part of natural scenery and are often employed by the poet as standards of comparison in his similes. It is beyond the scope of the present work to attempt a detailed account of trees, plants, creepers, flowers, birds and animals variously described in Kālidāsa's works. However, a few important points in this connection are noted here. We have already mentioned above briefly some trees, plants, flowers, birds and animals of different regions of India described in Kālidāsa's works. Moreover, the foregoing description of the seasons, mountains, rivers and lakes gives us an idea of some trees, flowers, birds and animals included therein. In a single verse of the Megh. Kālidāsa describes the ornamental beauty of half a dozen flowers worn by the youthful ladies of Alakā on their person :[46] "The young women of Alakā hold in their hands a lotus for sport. Their curly locks of hair are interwoven with budding jasmine flowers. Their faces look beautifully white with the pollen of *Lodhra* flowers. The knot of hair on their heads is adorned with fresh and lovely *Kurabaka* flowers, their ears with *Śirīṣa* flowers, and the parting-line of hair on their heads with *Kadamba* flowers." In pursuance of the poetical convention that an *Aśoka* tree blossoms only when it is struck by a beautiful maiden with her foot, Kālidāsa fondly describes the Aśoka tree with reference to beautiful maidens.[47] The elephant is described by Kālidāsa in various contexts as well as in numerous similes as a standard of comparison.[48] For instance, a cloud is compared to an elephant,[49] King Dilīpa to a tusker,[50] King Dilīpa and his Queen Sudakṣiṇā to a pair of celestial elephants called *Airāvata*,[51] and young Raghu to a baby elephant.[52] Similarly the cow, the bull and the deer also figure in some similes of Kālidāsa. The peacock,[53] the flamingo,[54] the *Chakravāka*,[55] the *Chātaka*,[56] the cuckoo,[57] the *Chakora*[58] (the Greek partridge), the crane,[59] and the *Kurarī*[60] (the female osprey) are some of the important birds which are poetically described in Kālidāsa's works. According to the poetic convention, the *Chātaka* is believed to drink only raindrops from a cloud and no other water; the *Chakora* is fabled to subsist on the rays of the moon; and a pair of the *Chakravākas*, supposed to be separated at night, is regarded as a symbol of conjugal fidelity.

The beauty of Kālidāsa's poetry is appreciably enhanced by the charming descriptions of clouds, the moon and the moonlit night in various ways. His lyric poem, the Megh., is devoted entirely to the fascinating description of a cloud journeying over various regions of India. The second Canto of the *Ṛtusaṃhāra* describes the natural scenery of the rainy season. The moon is a very popular standard of comparison which forms the basis of a large number of similes employed by the poet. Similarly the beauty of the star-lit night adorned with the rising moon is also described by Kālidāsa in his similes (*see* Notes 19 and 23 of Chapter V).

In short Kālidāsa whose poetic genius is inspired by Nature

describes the various aspects of Indian scenery in his inimitable, original and charming style.

It is a characteristic feature of Kālidāsa's description of Nature that he describes only the beautiful, charming and agreeable aspects of Nature and overlooks its sublime, sombre and dreadful aspects. Another noteworthy feature of Kālidāsa's treatment of Nature is that he invests it with human feelings. For instance, he imagines that like human beings Nature is also filled with amorous feelings in Spring. Therefore, on the advent of Spring with Cupid in the Himalayan forest of Śiva's hermitage the trees embraced, with their arms in the form of their stooping branches, their wives, creepers, which had breasts in the form of abundant bunches of flowers and charming lips in the form of quivering leaves.[61] It is said by the poet in the Ragh. that when Sītā, who was abandoned by Lakṣmaṇa in the forest near Vālmīki's hermitage, cried piteously, the entire Nature was grieved in sympathy with her. So the peacocks stopped their dance, the trees shed flowers, and the doe dropped the morsels of Darbha grass from their mouths.[62] In Act IV of the Śak. Kālidāsa vividly describes the feelings of sympathy in Nature at the time of Śakuntalā's departure for Hastināpura. In token of their good wishes for Śakuntalā the sylvan deities presented to her, with their sprout-like hands revealed up to the wrist from trees, an auspicious white silken garment, liquid lac-dye for painting her feet, and ornaments.[63] The trees of the hermitage bade her farewell through a cuckoo's note coming from the grove.[64] There was so much sorrow in Nature at the time of Śakuntalā's departure from the hermitage that the doe dropped from their mouths the morsels of Darbha grass, the peacocks stopped their dance, and the creepers seemed to shed tears in the form of their pale leaves.[65]

Kālidāsa seems to have drawn inspiration from Vālmīki, the first Classical poet (*Ādi-Kavi*), in delineating the sympathetic aspect of Nature ; for, the *Rāmāyaṇa* contains some descriptions of this type. For instance, Vālmīki depicts the entire Nature in sympathy with Sītā when she weeps pathetically at the time of her abduction by Rāvaṇa after Jaṭāyu's death in his fight against the demon King. Vālmīki imagines that at the abduction of Sītā the mountains, with their arms uplifted in the form of peaks, seemed to shed tears in the form of waterfalls ; the majestic sun with its pale orb appeared to be depressed; all the creatures wept in sympathy with her; and the frightened and depressed fawns cried in agony.[66]

Notes and References

1. दूरादयश्चक्रनिभस्य तन्वी तमालतालीवनराजिनीला ।
आभाति वेला लवणाम्बुराशेर्धारानिबद्धेव कलंकरेखा ।।
(Ragh. XIII, 15)

2. एषा प्रसन्नस्तिमितप्रवाहा सरिद्विदूरान्तरभावतन्वी ।
मन्दाकिनी भाति नगोपकण्ठे मुक्तावली कण्ठगतेव भूमेः ।।
(Ragh. XIII, 48)

3. Ragh. XIII, 54-55. Mallinātha explains *Kādamba* as *Nīlahaṃsa* "a blue goose."

4. शैलानामवरोहतीव शिखरादुन्मज्जतां मेदिनी
पर्णस्वान्तरलीनतां विजहति स्कन्धोदयात्पादपाः ।
संतानैस्तनुभावनष्टसलिला व्यक्तिं भजन्त्यापगाः
केनाप्युत्क्षिपतेव पश्य भुवनं मत्पाश्वंमानीयते ।।
(Śak. VII, 8)

5. मृगाः प्रचण्डातपतापिता भृशं
तृषा महत्या परिशुष्कतालवः ।
वनान्तरे तोयमिति प्रधाविता
निरीक्ष्य भिन्नांजनसंनिभं नभः ।।
(RS. I, 11)

6. श्वसिति विहगवर्गः शीर्णपर्णद्रुमस्थः
कपिकुलमुपयाति क्लान्तमद्रेर्निकुंजम् ।
भ्रमति गवययूथः सर्वतस्तोयमिच्छञ्
छरभकुलमजिह्मं प्रोद्धरत्यम्बु कूपात् ।।
(RS. I, 23)

7. विपाण्डुरं कीटरजस्तृणान्वितं
भुजंगवद् वक्रगतिप्रसर्पितम् ।

ससाध्वसैर्भेककुलैर्निरीक्षितं

प्रयाति निम्नाभिमुखं नवोदकम् ।।

(RS. II, 13)

8. ग्रीवाभंगाभिरामं मुहुरनुपतति स्यन्दने बद्धदृष्टि:

पश्चार्धेन प्रविष्ट: शरपतनभयाद् भूयसा पूर्वकायम् ।

दर्भैरर्धावलीढै: श्रमविवृतमुखभ्रंशिभि: कीर्णवर्त्मा

पश्योदग्रप्लुतत्वाद् वियति बहुतरं स्तोकमुर्व्यां प्रयाति ।।

(Śak. I, 7)

9. KS. VIII, 28 seq.

10. There are divergent views about the identification of Mount *Hemakūṭa*. Some scholars are inclined to identify it with Mount *Kailāsa*; cf. B.S. Upadhyaya, *India in Kālidāsa*, p. 4. But according to another view, the *Hemakūṭa* is situated to the north of the Himalayas and forms the boundaries of the *Kinnara* or *Kiṃpuruṣa Varṣa*; cf., Monier Williams, *Sanskrit-English Dictionary, s.v.* According to the Mbh. (III, 110, 1-18), the *Hemakūṭa* alias *Ṛṣabhakūṭa* is the abode of the gods, which is inaccessible to ordinary people and where the voice of Vedic recitation is heard but no reciter is visible.

11. जलधरविनतानामाश्रयोऽस्माकमुच्चै-

रयमिति जलसेकैस्तोयदास्तोयनम्रा: ।

अतिशयपरुषाभिर्ग्रीष्मवह्ने: शिखाभि:

समुपजनिततापं ह्लादयन्तीव विन्ध्यम् ।।

(RS. II, 27)

12. Ibid. II, 8. Some MSS. read *ramyāṇi* instead of *Vaindhyāni*.

13. बाष्पसारा हेमकाञ्चीगुणेन श्रोणीबिम्बादप्युपेक्षाच्युतेन ।

चण्डी चण्डं हन्तुमभ्युद्यता मां विद्युद्दाम्ना मेघराजीव विन्ध्यम् ।।

(Māl. III, 21)

14. Ragh. XII, 31.

15. Ibid. XIV, 8.

16. धारास्वनोद्गारिदरीमुखोऽसौ शृंगाग्रलग्नाम्बुदवप्रपंक: ।

बध्नाति मे बन्धुरगात्रि ! चक्षुर्दृप्त: ककुद्मानिव चित्रकूट: ।।

(Ragh. XIII, 47)

17. Ragh. XIII, 10.

18. मातंगनक्रै: सहसोत्पतद्भिर्भिन्नान्द्विधा पश्य समुद्रफेनान् ।

कपोलसंसर्पितया य एषां व्रजन्ति कर्णक्षणचामरत्वम् ।।

(Ragh. XIII, 11)

19. Ibid. XIII, 12.

20. Ibid. XIII, 13.

21. Ibid. XIII, 14.
22. Ibid. XIII, 17.
23. Ibid. II, 3.
24. RS. II, 7.
25. Ibid. III, 3.
26 तां हंसमालाः शरदीव गंगां महौषधिं नक्तमिवात्मभासः ।
स्थिरोपदेशामुपदेशकाले प्रपेदिरे प्राक्तनजन्मविद्याः ॥
(KS. I, 30)
27. KS. I, 54.
28. Ibid. VI, 38.
29. Pūrvamegha, 50 (*see* Note 8 of Chapter I).
30. Ibid. 51.
31. Ibid. 63.
32. Uttaramegha, 4.
33. Ragh. IV, 32.
34. Ibid. X, 26.
35. Ibid. X, 69.
36. Ibid. XIII, 60-63.
37. Ibid. XVI, 54-71.
38. Ibid. VI, 35.
39. Pūrvamegha, 31.
40. Ibid. 19.
41. त्वय्यादातुं जलमवनते शार्ङ्गिणो वर्णचौरे
तस्याः सिन्धोः पृथुमपि तनुं दूरभावात्प्रवाहम् ।
प्रेक्षिष्यन्ते गगनगतयो नूनमावर्ज्य दृष्टी-
रेकं मुक्तागुणमिव भुवः स्थूलमध्येन्द्रनीलम् ॥
(Pūrvamegha, 46)
42. RS. III, 11; cf. Ragh. I, 43; VI, 86.
43. प्रफुल्लनीलोत्पलशोभितानि
सोन्मादकादम्बविभूषितानि ।
प्रसन्नतोयानि सुशीतलानि
सरांसि चेतांसि हरन्ति पुंसाम् ॥
(RS. IV, 9)
44. Pūrvamegha, 62; Uttaramegha, 13; KS. VIII, 64; Ragh. VI, 26; XIII, 60.
45. Ragh. XIII, 30; cf. R. IV, 1.
46. हस्ते लीलाकमलमलके बालकुन्दानुविद्धं
नीता लोध्रप्रसवरजसा पाण्डुतामानने श्रीः ।

चूडापाशे नवकुरबकं चारु कर्णे शिरीषं
सीमन्ते च त्वदुपगमजं यत्र नीपं वधूनाम् ।।
(Uttaramegha, 2)

47. KS. III, 26; Māl. III, 12. 17; Ragh. VIII, 62; RS. VI, 16.
48. RS. VI, 28; Pūrvamegha, 19; Ragh. II, 7; III, 37; XVI, 16.
49. RS. II, 1; Pūrvamegha, 2.
50. Ragh. III, 3.
51. Ibid. I, 36.
52. Ibid. III, 32.
53. RS. I, 13; Pūrvamegha, 22.32.44; Uttaramegha, 16. 41; Ragh. II, 17; etc.
54. RS. I, 5; III, 2; Pūrvamegha, 11. 23; KS. I, 30; Ragh. IV, 19; etc.
55. KS. VII, 15; VIII, 32; Ragh. III, 24; XIII, 31; etc.
56. RS. II, 3; Pūrvamegha, 9; Uttaramegha, 51; Ragh. V, 17; etc.
57. RS. VI, 14. 20-22.27; KS. III, 32; IV, 14; Vik. IV, 56; Śak. V, 22; VI, 4; etc.
58. Ragh. VI, 59; VII, 25; etc.
59. RS. I, 19; III, 8.12.16; Pūrvamegha, 9.31; Ragh. XIII, 30.33; etc.
60. Ragh. XIV, 68; Vik. p. 9; etc.
61. पर्याप्तपुष्पस्तबकस्तनाभ्यः स्फुरत्प्रवालौष्ठमनोहराभ्यः ।
लतावधूभ्यस्तरवोऽप्यवापुर्विनम्रशाखाभुजबन्धनानि ।।
(KS. III, 39)
62. नृत्यं मयूराः कुसुमानि वृक्षा दर्भानुपात्तान्विजहुर्हरिण्यः ।
तस्याः प्रपन्ने समदुःखभावमत्यन्तमासीद्रुदितं वनेऽपि ।।
(Ragh. XIV, 69)
63. Śak. IV, 4.
64. Ibid. IV, 9.
65. उद्गलितदर्भकवला मृग्यः परित्यक्तनर्तना मयूराः ।
अपसृतपाण्डुपत्रा मुञ्चन्त्यश्रूणीव लताः ।।
(Śak. IV, 11)
66. R. III, 52, 39-42.

7

Kālidāsa's Concept of Beauty and Love

Kālidāsa perceives beauty in every particle of the universe and vividly portrays it in his inimitable and charming style. Like Śiva who swallowed poison churned out of the ocean for the welfare of the world, Kālidāsa swallows ugliness and unpleasantness and offers only beauty and delight to his readers. So he describes in his poetry the beauty of heaven and earth, of the moon and seasons, of night and dawn, of clouds and lightning, of mountains and forests, of lakes and rivers, of trees and creepers, of sprouts and flowers, of birds and animals, and of bees and insects, as discussed above in Chapter VI. Kālidāsa conceives the beauty of Nature in terms of human sentiments. For instance, he imagines a star-lit night with the rising moon as a beautiful young bride adorned with ornaments (see Notes 19 and 23 of Chapter V). He conceives the ripples of a mountain stream as the movements of Urvaśī's eyebrows, and its meandering current as her stumbling gait.[1] The poet imagines the quivering leaves of creepers to be their charming lips and the abundant bunches of flowers to be their breasts in relation to their lovers, trees, who hug them with their arms in the form of their stooping branches.[2] Kālidāsa conceives the earth, covered with the blossoming *Kiṃśuka* trees resembling conflagration in Spring, as a beautiful young bride clad in a red raiment.[3] In the eyes of the poet the beauty of Nature is an integral part of human beauty, and he sees in Nature the standards of comparison to describe human beauty. For instance, he generally compares a beautiful maiden's face to the moon, her eyes to the blue lotuses or to the eyes of a gazelle, the movements of her eye-brows to the ripples of water in a river, her tresses to the feathers of a peacock, her lower lip to the ripe *Bimba* fruit, her thighs to the trunk of an elephant or to the stem of a plantain tree, her feet to the flowers of a ground lotus (Hibiscus Mutabilis : *Sthalārvinda*), and her gait to that of a flamingo. In order to depict the extraordinary beauty of Umā, Kālidāsa imagines that her beauty is far superior to the conventional standards of natural beauty. Therefore, the poet says that her arms are more tender than a *Śirīṣa* flower ;[4] and that the face of Umā combines in itself the beauty of both the moon and the lotus, while the moon is devoid of the beauty of the lotus and the latter lacks the lustre of the former.[5] Similarly Kālidāsa imagines that if either a flower be placed on a tender sprout or a pearl be placed on a crystal clear coral, such a combination may resemble the charming and graceful smile on Umā's cherry lips.[6]

Kālidāsa minutely describes in his works[7] the perfect form, proportionate limbs, attractive features and charming qualities of beautiful maidens. He considers beauty to be a unique artistic creation of the Creator. On seeing the voluptuous beauty of Urvaśī, King Purūravas thinks that for her creation the beautifying moon, or Cupid himself embodying the erotic sentiment, or the vernal month abounding in flowers seems to have assumed the role of the Creator; and the King wonders how the old sage (*Brahman*), whose senses have been dulled by the constant recitation of the Vedas and who is averse to sensual pleasures, could have created this enchanting beauty.[8] Describing the peerless beauty of Śakuntalā to his companion Māṭhavya, King Duṣyanta says that she seems to have been created by the Creator through his mental power with the aggregate of entire beauty of the universe, after painting her picture first and then investing it with life ; and that she appears to be the matchless model (lit. creation) of a most beautiful woman in view of the Creator's omnipotence and her lovely form.[9] A similar idea is contained in the KS. which says that the Creator created Umā with great effort by appropriately apportioning to her limbs the beauty of all the natural standards of comparison, with a view to beholding entire beauty amassed in a single form, as it were.[10]

Although Kālidāsa often describes ornaments and flowers used by women for decoration, yet he holds the view that natural beauty which needs no adornment turns even a bark-garment into a decorative dress. King Duşyanta who first sights Śakuntalā in a bark-garment is charmed by her natural beauty and observes :[11] "Even the bark-garment, which obviously does not suit her young age, enhances her beauty ; for, as the lotus even intermixed with moss looks beautiful, and even the black spot adds to the beauty of the moon, so this slender maiden appears to be more lovely even in the bark-garment. What is not an ornament for charming forms ?"

Kālidāsa does not confine his view to skin-deep beauty and lays great stress on noble and spiritual qualities of character. For instance, Śiva in the guise of a Brahmachārin tells Pārvatī that the maxim that a beautiful form never commits a sin holds good in her case, as her conduct is worthy of emulation even by the ascetics.[12] All the beautiful ladies characterized in Kālidāsa's works are possessed of high, noble and spiritual qualities. Pārvatī and Sītā are goddesses in human form. Urvaśī is a heavenly nymph who travels from heaven to earth and vice versa. Śakuntalā is the daughter of the sage Viśvāmitra and the nymph Menakā. Aja's wife Indumatī was a nymph who had to take birth as a woman on account of a curse. So all these ladies are shown as endowed with divine qualities and free from human frailties. Mālavikā is depicted as an accomplished and cultured princess.

In spite of sensuous description of beauty in his works Kālidāsa disapproves of sensuality and depicts the lofty ideal of pure, sincere and lasting conjugal love. According to the poet, the only usefulness of a woman's beauty is to win the heart of her husband.[13] He deprecates sensual passion arising from mere physical attraction without mutual love between the lover and the beloved. So when King Agnimitra overhears Mālavikā's confession of love for him in her conversation with Bakulāvalikā, he feels delighted and says to the Vidūşaka :[14] "Friend ! the object of the lovers is achieved by this much. I see no pleasure in the union of those persons one of whom is cold and the other is passionate. On the contrary, I prefer to such an insipid union the death of two true lovers who are equally in love with each other but are despaired of their union." Both the hero and the heroine in all the three plays of Kālidāsa are shown equally in love with each other since their first meeting.

The deplorable exploitation of beauty to seduce sages, ascetics, virtuous men and chaste women is exposed by the poet through the bragging of Cupid who boastfully claims infallible power to seduce not only mortals but also Lord Śiva famed for self-control.[15] But Cupid fails in his mission and is reduced to ashes when he tries secretly to influence the mind of Lord Śiva. By first giving a vivid description of Umā's ravishing beauty and then by showing its futility to entice Śiva, Kālidāsa conveys the message that great minds are impervious to the ensnaring charm of physical beauty which allures ordinary mortals. According to Kālidāsa's ideal of a balanced and virtuous life, the enjoyment of pleasures (*Kāma*) must be regulated by the consideration of righteous conduct (*Dharma*) as ordained by Lord Kṛṣṇa in the *Bhagavadgītā* ;[16] and unbridled indulgence in sensual pleasures due to only physical attraction in violation of the code of ethical conduct leads to sin and miseries, as illustrated by the poet in the case of Agnivarṇa in Canto XIX of the Ragh. This ideal forms the corner-stone of Kālidāsa's conception of pure, sincere and lasting love.

In the KS. Kālidāsa depicts two different phases of Umā's love for Śiva. In the earlier phase she sought to win Śiva's heart by her physical charm. In the gaieties of the vernal season produced by Cupid to seduce Śiva at Indra's behest when Umā went to Śiva and offered him a rosary of the seeds of Gangetic lotuses, he felt a bit excited like the ocean at the rising of the moon, and cast a covetous glance at her beautiful face charming with the *Bimba*-like lower lip.[17] But Śiva soon controlled his passion, looked around to find out the cause of his excitement, spotted Cupid ready to discharge an arrow at him, reduced him to ashes, and vanished from the scene.[18] Finding her beauty futile to win Śiva, Umā returned home in despair.

Realising the truth that mere physical charm is not enough to win the love of high-minded persons, she sought to achieve her object by cultivating in herself spiritual qualities through austerities and meditation ; for there was no other way to obtain such a husband and his lasting love.[19] This is the later and higher phase of Umā's love for Śiva. In pursuance of her resolve she practised austerities to such an extent that she excelled even the renowned ascetics in this respect. Her spotless deeds were declared by Śiva to be more purifying than the celestial waters of the Gaṅgā.[20] In the garb of a Brahmachārin Śiva tested the intensity and sincerity of her love by praising her charming beauty in contrast to his own dreadful ugly appearance. But she remained steadfast in her love and asserted emphatically :[21] "There is no need of any argumentation. Let him be such in entirety as heard by you. But my mind, delighting solely in the sentiment of love, is exclusively devoted to him ; and one, who is free to act according to one's will, does not care for reproach." Umā's constant and sincere love, purified by her meditation and austerities and ennobled by her spiritual qualities, ultimately won the heart of Śiva who had previously spurned mere physical beauty. Revealing his true identity, Śiva then told Umā that thenceforth he was her slave purchased with her austerities.

Kālidāsa is of the view that pure, sincere and lasting love, which is free from blind passion and rashness, should be consecrated by the due performance of nuptials and cemented by irrevocable conjugal relationship to conduce to happy family life and social welfare. Therefore, Umā who had to bear so much agony and hardship to win Śiva's heart did not rush to him passionately on receiving his positive response. She conveyed her desire to Śiva through a friend that her father (*Himālaya*) should be requested to give her away in marriage to him. Śiva accepted her proposal and their marriage was duly solemnized. At the time of their wedding the officiating priest advised Umā :[22] "Dear daughter ! this sacred Fire is a witness to your act of marriage. You should unhesitatingly perform your religious duties in conjunction with your husband Śiva." In keeping with this advice Kālidāsa observes elsewhere that the performance of religious duties in a household depends entirely on a virtuous wife.[23] The bond of marriage is regarded by the poet as a sacred brake on the fast-moving vehicle of youthful pleasures (*Kāma*), the destination of which is a happy family life fructifying into good progeny. Therefore, the birth of *Kumāra* (*Kārttikeya*), who delivers the world from the tyrannies of the demon Tāraka, is considered by Kālidāsa to be the main aim of the union of Śiva and Pārvatī : hence the title "*Kumāra-Sambhava*" (the birth of Kumāra) of this epic.

It has been shown by the poet in his lyrical poem *Meghadūta* that negligence in the performance of duties on account of excessive indulgence in sensual pleasures results in suffering and agony. The Yakṣa, who was exiled for a year for neglecting hit duties, had to suffer the pangs of separation from his dear wife. The mind of a separated lover is so much distracted that he fails to distinguish between animate and inanimate objects at the time of giving expression to his intense feeling of love. So the exiled Yakṣa chose a cloud as his messenger to convey to his separated wife the message of his deep love. It shows that sincere love becomes more intense in separation; and that the reunion of separated lovers brings in greater happiness. In the Megh. Kālidāsa shows his mastery in delineating the sentiment of love in separation.

Different stages of love are depicted in the Vik. King Purūravas and the celestial nymph Urvaśī fall in love at first sight. At the time of her going away to heaven Urvaśī turns back to see the King on the pretext of disentangling her necklace entangled in a creeper. On her departure for heaven King Purūravas feels that this nymph, flying in the sky, forcibly tears away his mind from his body like a goose which pulls out a fibre from the broken tip of the root of a lotus.[24] Both the lover and the beloved pine for each other. On the Vidūṣaka's suggestion to seek union with her in a dream or in a painting, Purūravas says that it is not possible for him to get sleep as his heart is pierced with the arrows of love; nor can he unite himself with her in a painting, because his sight is obstructed with tears before he could complete her picture in a painting.[25] Expressing her feeling of intense love for Purūravas, Urvaśī says that on account of his separation from her the pleasant breeze of Indra's garden seems to torment, like fire, her body lying on the bed of soft flowers of the celestial tree called *Pārijāta*.[26] Moreover, Urvaśī is so much enamoured of Purūravas that during the performance of a play in heaven she unconsciously utters the name of her lover Pururavas instead of Puruṣottama, while she is playing the role of Lakṣmī. Their union after a period of intense longing for each other is described by Kālidāsa as a more delightful pleasure following tribulation, like the comfort enjoyed in the shade of a tree by a person parched by the sun.[27]

Then it is shown by Kālidāsa that passionate love leading to excessive indulgence in sensual pleasures results in miseries. When Purūravas and Urvaśī were enjoying amorous sports in the Gandhamādana forest on the peak of Mount Kailāsa, she suspected his fidelity for his looking at a Vidyādhara girl playing there and was transformed into a creeper after she had angrily entered Kumāra's penance-grove prohibited to women. Purūravas became almost insane owing to the grief of her separation and roamed about in the forest like a mad person enquiring about her whereabouts from trees, birds, animals, mountains and rivers. Their reunion is brought about by only a miracle to indicate that such a reunion is rare. When her son Āyus who was secretly handed over by Urvaśī to the sage Chyavana for upbringing is brought before King Purūravas by an old ascetic lady, Urvaśī and Purūravas are again faced with the threat of permanent separation in pursuance of a curse. The gloomy prospects of their permanent separation make Urvaśī weep bitterly and Purūravas fall into a swoon. The King decides to retire to the forest in despair after entrusting the reins of administration to his son Āyus. It is again Indra's intervention which saves the lovers from permanent separation. However, it is worth noting that the sage Nārada who brings Indra's message says that Purūravas should not renounce his arms and that Urvaśī should live with him for life as his lawful wife for the performance of religious duties.[28] Kālidāsa intends to show through his play Vik. that love based on mere physical charm stumbles from one pitfall into another and cannot give enduring happiness; and that only the sense of moral duty on the part of lovers can form the basis of pure, sincere and life-long love.

In his masterpiece, *Śākuntala*, Kālidāsa first delineates the gross passionate aspect of love between Duṣyanta and Śakuntalā and then its sublimation into pure spiritual love. Both fall in love at first sight and unite secretly according to the *Gāndharva* form of marriage which is based on mutual love.[28a] Their secret union results in her pregnancy. Having come to know of her secret marriage with Duṣyanta, her foster-father Kaṇva on his return to his hermitage significantly tells her :[29] "The oblation of the sacrificer, whose sight was obstructed by smoke, fell fortunately into the sacrificial fire." The implication of this remark is that though her judgment to unite secretly with King Duṣyanta was blinded by passion yet she fortunately got a worthy match. On account of her passionate love for Duṣyanta Śakuntalā remained lost in her thought about him all the time and consequently became guilty of derelection of moral duty towards an honoured guest, which infuriated the irascible sage Durvāsas to pronounce the curse that her lover in whose thought she was absorbed would forget her. On the entreaties of her friend Priyaṃvadā Durvāsas relented that the King would recognize Śakuntalā on showing him some ornament as a token of recognition. In order to demonstrate the adverse consequences of ephemeral love born out of gross passion, Kālidāsa introduces the episode of loss of the recognition ring, which leads to the repudiation of Śakuntalā and simultaneously absolves Duṣyanta from the blame of repudiating his lawful wife. The loss of the ring symbolizes the end of the passionate love.

The recovery of the lost ring marks a turning-point in the development of spiritual love between Duṣyanta and Śakuntalā. The King then regains his past memory and constantly repents his wrongful action in repudiating Śakuntalā. He bans the celebration of vernal festival, pines for her day and night, cannot sleep at night, and paints her picture which he is unable to behold fully on account of the obstruction of his sight with tears (*see* Note 25). He becomes emaciated due to ceaseless agony. He laments his own childlessness and the repudiation of Śakuntalā who was to bear him an offspring, when he is informed by his minister about the death of an issueless merchant. The King displays his kindness towards his subjects by proclaiming that excepting immoral relationship he himself would be the relative of those who are bereaved of any near and dear one ; and that the property of the deceased merchant should go to the prospective child of his expectant wife. Thus Duṣyanta's repentence for his wrongful repudiation of Śakuntalā has spiritually elevated him and sublimated his love. Śakuntalā, who was taken away by her mother Menakā after repudiation by the King, gave birth to a son in the hermitage of the sage Mārīcha and began to lead the austere life of a chaste lady separated from her husband. In the course of his return journey to his Capital from heaven after aiding Indra in vanquishing demons, Duṣyanta visits the sage Mārīcha's hermitage and happens to meet there his son Sarvadamana who becomes instrumental in the reunion of Duṣyanta and Śakuntalā. Kālidāsa has thoughtfully constructed the plot of the play in such a way as to bring about the reunion of the lovers through their progeny which is undoubtedly an unbreakable bond of unity between father and mother. At the time of their reunion Śakuntalā, wearing faded garments and keeping her hair tied in a single knot, looks emaciated, and Duṣyanta is also a changed man due to his constant repentence. He begs her forgiveness, while she blames her own previous deeds for her miseries. Both are spiritually elevated. Their first meeting was full of passion, but their reunion is the result of their sincere love purified by repentence and austerities. The physical token of recognition which played such an important part in the vicissitudes of their love ceases to have any significance after their spiritual reunion. Therefore, Śakuntalā refuses to accept and trust the recognition ring when Duṣyanta offers it to her. The sage Mārīcha advises her not to feel offended with her husband, because the curse was the real cause of her insult and humiliation. Kālidāsa's concept of pure and lasting conjugal love is expressed in the words of the sage Mārīcha who figuratively describes a virtuous wife (Śakuntalā), a noble husband (Duṣyanta) and good progeny (Sarvadamana) as faith, sacred injunction and prosperity respectively.[30]

Although Kālidāsa's delineation of love in the Ragh. is circumscribed to a large extent by the epic tradition inherited by him, he misses no opportunity to express his own ideal of love. Indumatī who chose Aja as her husband at a *Svayaṃvara* was intensely loved by him. It is said by the poet that Indumatī's choice naturally fell on her worthy match Aja among a large number of kings present there, because the mind knows the past association of previous births.[31] Aja's love for Indumatī was so deep that after her accidental death he wailed piteously as described below by the poet :[32] "Giving up his innate courage, Aja wailed aloud with his voice choked by sobs. Even iron melts in fire, what to speak of mortals?" In his wailing he mournfully remembered Indumatī not only as his beloved wife but also as his counsellor, confidante and dearest pupil in every fine art.[33] It is said in the Ragh. that King Aja lamented for his dear wife so pathetically that his poignant pathos moved even the trees to tears of sorrowful sympathy.[34] Nothing could mitigate his grief. He remained grief-stricken and disconsolate for eight long years after which he handed over the kingdom to his son Daśaratha and left his mortal frame at the confluence of the sacred rivers Gaṅgā and Sarayū to seek lasting union with Indumatī in heaven.

In depicting the ideal conjugal love of Rāma and Sītā, Kālidāsa is mostly indebted to Vālmīki. However, Kālidāsa shows his originality in the wording of the message sent by Sītā to Rāma through Lakṣmaṇa after her abandonment in the forest. Describing the high character of Sītā, Kālidāsa informs us that she did not utter even a word of reproach against Rāma who had abandoned her, knowing her to be pure. Instead she attributed her misfortune to her own previous deeds, and expressed her desire to have him again as her husband in the next birth also.[35] Rāma, who sacrificed his love for the sake of his duty towards his subjects, burst into tears on hearing her message, because he had expelled Sītā from his house for fear of any blemish attaching to the reputation of his family, but not from his heart.[36] Rāma always cherished Sītā's love and carried out his duties with a heavy heart. He took Sītā's golden statue as his partner in the performance of the Aśvamedha sacrifice. When Sītā was brought before Rāma by Vālmīki to convince the people about her purity, she prayed to the goddess Earth :[37] "O Goddess Earth ! take me in thy bosom, if I have never been unfaithful to my husband in word, thought and deed." As soon as she uttered these words, a halo of light appeared from an opening of the earth and disappeared into the earth after taking away Sītā. The character of Rāma and Sītā represents the highest ideal of unflinching conjugal love. Neither Sītā can think of another man under any circumstances nor can Rāma dream of another woman in any case.

Notes and References

1. Vik. IV. 52.
2. KS. III, 39 (*see* Note 61 of Chapter VI).
3. RS. VI, 19 (*see* Note 25 of Chapter V).
4. KS. I, 41.
5. चन्द्रं गता पद्मगुणान्न भुंक्ते पद्माश्रिता चान्द्रमसीमभिख्याम्।
   उमामुखं नु प्रतिपद्य लोला द्विसंश्रयां प्रीतिमवाप लक्ष्मीः ।।
   (KS. I, 43)
6. पुष्पं प्रवालोपहितं यदि स्यान्मुक्ताफलं वा स्फुटविद्रुमस्थम् ।
   ततोऽनुकुर्याद्विशदस्य तस्यास्ताम्रौष्ठपर्यस्तरुचः स्मितस्य ।।
   (KS. I, 44)
7. Māl. II, 3 (*see* Chapter IV, Mālavikā); Uttaramegha, 19; Śak. I, 18; KS. I, 32-48.
8. अस्याः सर्गविधौ प्रजापतिरभूच्चन्द्रो नु कान्तिप्रदः
   शृंगारैकरसः स्वयं नु मदनो मासो नु पुष्पाकरः ।
   वेदाभ्यासजडः कथं नु विषयव्यावृत्तकौतुहलो
   निर्मातुं प्रभवेन्मनोहरमिदं रूपं पुराणो मुनिः ।।
   (Vik. I, 10)
9. Śak. II, 9. Some MSS. read *chitte* instead of the initial word *chitre* and some scholars explain *Strī-ratnasṛṣtir aparā* as "another creation of a beautiful woman" or "the creation of another gem as a beauty besides the fourteen gems mythologically believed to be churned out of the ocean by the gods."
10. सर्वोपमाद्रव्यसमुच्चयेन यथाप्रदेशं विनिवेशितेन ।
    सा निर्मिता विश्वसृजा प्रयत्नादेकस्थसौन्दर्यदिदृक्षयेव ।।
    (KS. I, 49)
11. काममननुरूपमस्या वयसो वल्कलं न पुनरलंकारश्रियं न पुष्यति । कुतः ?
    सरसिजमनुविद्धं शैवलेनापि रम्यं
    मलिनमपि हिमांशोर्लक्ष्म लक्ष्मीं तनोति ।
    इयमधिकमनोज्ञा वल्कलेनापि तन्वी
    किमिव हि मधुराणां मण्डनं नाकृतीनाम् ।।
    (Śak. I, 17)

12. यदुच्यते पार्वति ! पापवृत्तये न रूपमित्यव्यभिचारि तद्वचः ।
तथा हि ते शीलमुदारदर्शने ! तपस्विनामप्युपदेशतां गतम् ॥
(KS. V, 36)

13. प्रियेषु सौभाग्यफला हि चारुता
(KS. V, 1)

14. Māl. III, 15.
15. KS. III, 3-10.
16. धर्माविरूद्धो भूतेषु कामोऽस्मि भरतर्षभ ।
(Bh. G. VII, 11)
न धर्ममर्थकामाभ्यां बबाधे न च तेन तौ ।
नार्थं कामेन कामं वा सोऽर्थेन सदृशस्त्रिषु ॥
(Ragh. XVII, 57)

17. KS. III, 65-67.
18. Ibid. III, 69-74.
19. इयेष सा कर्तुमवन्ध्यरूपतां समाधिमास्थाय तपोभिरात्मनः ।
अवाप्यते वा कथमन्यथा द्वयं तथाविधं प्रेम पतिश्च तादृशः ॥
(KS. V, 2)

20. KS. V, 37.
21. अलं विवादेन यथाश्रुतस्त्वया तथाविधस्तावदशेषमस्तु सः ।
ममात्र भावैकरसं मनः स्थितं न कामवृत्तिर्वचनीयमीक्षते ॥
(KS. V, 82)

22. वधूं द्विजः प्राह तवैष वत्से ! वह्निर्विवाहं प्रति कर्मसाक्षी ।
शिवेन भर्त्रा सह धर्मचर्या कार्या त्वया मुक्तविचारयेति ॥
(KS. VII, 83)

23. क्रियाणां खलु धर्म्याणां सत्पत्न्यो मूलकारणम् ।
(KS. VI, 13)

24. Vik. I, 20 (*see* Note 24 of Chapter V).
25. Ibid. II, 10; cf. Uttaramegha, 42; Śak. VI, 22.
26. Ibid. II, 12.
27. यदेवोपनतं दुःखात्सुखं तद्रसवत्तरम् ।
निर्वाणाय तरुच्छाया तप्तस्य हि विशेषतः ॥
(Vik. III, 21)

28. Vik., p. 138—
तेन न त्वया शस्त्रन्यासः कर्तव्यः ।
इयं चोर्वशी यावदायुस्तव सहधर्मचारिणी भवत्विति ।

28a. See, *India of Vedic Kalpasūtras*, pp. 205-207.
29. Śak., p. 125—
दिष्ट्या धूमाकुलितदृष्टेरपि यजमानस्य पावक एवाहुतिः पतिता ।

30. दिष्ट्या शकुन्तला साध्वी सदपत्यमिदं भवान् ।
श्रद्धा वित्तं विधिश्चेति त्रितयं तत्समागतम् ॥

(Śak. VII, 29)

31. रतिस्मरौ (v.1. जातिस्मरौ) नूनमिमावभूतां राज्ञां सहस्रेषु तथा हि बाला ।
गतेयमात्मप्रतिरूपमेव मनो हि जन्मान्तरसंगतिज्ञम् ॥

(Ragh. VII, 15)

32. विललाप स बाष्पगद्गदं सहजामप्यपहाय धीरताम् ।
अभितप्तमयोऽपि मार्दवं भजते कैव कथा शरीरिषु ॥

(Ragh. VIII, 43)

33. गृहिणी सचिवः सखी मिथः प्रियशिष्या ललिते कलाविधौ ।
करुणाविमुखेन मृत्युना हरता त्वां वद किं न मे हृतम् ॥

(Ragh. VIII, 67)

34. विलपन्निति कोसलाधिपः करुणार्थग्रथितं प्रियां प्रति ।
अकरोत्पृथिवीरुहानपि स्रुतशाखारसबाष्पदूषितान् ॥

(Ragh. VIII, 70)

35. Ibid. XIV, 57-67.

36. बभूव रामः सहसा सबाष्पस्तुषारवर्षीव सहस्यचन्द्रः ।
कौलीनभीतेन गृहान्निरस्ता न तेन वैदेहसुता मनस्तः ॥

(Ragh. XIV, 84)

37. वाङ्मनःकर्मभिः पत्यौ व्यभिचारो यथा न मे ।
तथा विश्वंभरे देवि ! मामन्तर्धातुमर्हसि ॥

(Ragh. XV, 81)

SELECT BIBLIOGRAPHY

I. The Epics

1. *Mahābhārata*: Gītā Press Gorakhpur, Saṃvat 2013-2015.
2. *Rāmāyaṇa of Vālmīki*: Ed. by K. Chinnaswami Sastriga and V.H. Subrahmanya Sastri, Madras, 2nd edition, 1958.

II. The Epic Poems of Kālidāsa

1. *Kumārasambhava* with Mallinātha's commentary: Ed. by Nārāyaṇa Rāma Āchārya, Nirnaya Sagar Press, Bombay, 14th edition, 1955.
2. *Raghuvaṃśa* with Mallinātha's commentary: Ed. by H.D. Velankar, Nirnaya Sagar Press, Bombay, 11th edition, 1948.

III. The Lyric Poems of Kālidāsa

1. *Ṛtusaṃhāra* with *Chandrikā* commentary of *Maṇirāma*: Ed. by Nārāyaṇa Rāma Āchārya, Nirnaya Sagar Press, Bombay, 8th edition, 1952.
2. *Meghadūta* with Mallinātha's commentary: Ed. by Nārāyaṇa Rāma Āchārya, Nirnaya Sagar Press, Bombay, 16th edition, 1953.

IV. The Plays of Kālidāsa

1. *Abhijñānaśākuntala* with the commentary of Rāghavabhaṭṭa: Ed. by Nārāyaṇa Rāma Āchārya, Nirnaya Sagar Press, Bombay, 11th edition, 1947.
2. *Mālavikāgnimitra* with the commentary of Kāṭayavema : Ed. by K.P. Parab, Nirnaya Sagar Press, Bombay, 8th edition, 1935.
3. *Vikramorvaśīya* with *Prakāśikā* commentary of Raṅganātha: Ed. by W.L. Pansikar, Nirnaya Sagar Press, Bombay, 6th edition, 1925.

V. Other Texts

1. *Agni Purāṇa*: Ānandāśrama, Poona, 1900.
2. *Amarakoṣa*: Ed. with Hindi Translation by Ramaswarupa Bholanath Pandit, Śrī Veṅkateṣwar Press, Bombay, 1895.
3. *Arthaśāstra of Kauṭilya*: Ed. with Hindi Translation by Udayavir Shastri, Lahore, 1925.
4. *Avantisundarī-kathā*: Ed. by K.S. Mahadeva Shastri, Trivandrum, 1954.
5. *Bhāgavata Purāṇa*: Gitā Press Gorakhpur, 1965.
6. *Bhāsa-nāṭaka-chakra*: Ed. by C.R. Devadhar, Poona, 1937.
7. *Brahma Purāṇa*: Ānandāśrama, Poona, 1895.
8. *Buddhacharita*: Ed. with English Translation by E.H. Johnston, Lahore, 1936.
   —— : Ed. by E.B. Cowell, Oxford, 1893.
9. *Daśakumāracharita*: Ed. by N.B Godbole, Nirnaya Sagar Press, Bombay, 14th edition, 1940.
10. *Harṣacharita*: Ed. by K.P. Parab, Nirnaya Sagar Press, Bombay, 7th edition, 1946.
11. *Kādambarī*: Ed. by M.R. Kale, Bombay, 3rd revised edition, 1928.
12. *Kālikā Purāṇa*: Śrī Veṅkateṣwar Press, Bombay, 1967.
13. *Kāmasūtra of Vātsyāyana*: Ed. by Goswami Damodar Shastri, Kashi Sanskrit Series, Benares, 1929.
14. *Kāvyādarśa*: Ed. with Sanskrit commentary and Hindi Translation by D.K. Gupta, Delhi, 1973.
15. *Kūrma Purāṇa*: Ed. by Anandasvarup Gupta, Varanasi, 1971.
16. *Matsya Purāṇa*: Ānandāśrama, Poona, 1907.
17. *Manusmṛti* with the commentary of Kulluka: Ed. by Nārāyaṇa Rāma Āchārya, 10th edition, Bombay, 1946.
18. *Padma Purāṇa*: Ānandāśrama, Poona, 1893-94.
19. *Sāhityadarpaṇa*: Ed. with Hindi Translation by Śālagrāma Śāstrī, Lucknow, 2nd edition, Saṃvat 1991.
20. *Saundarananda*: Ed. by H.P. Shastri, Calcutta, 1939. (re-issue edition with additions by Chintaharan Chakravarti).
    —— : critical edition with notes by E.H. Johnston, 1928; English Translation, 1932 (Oxford University Press).
21. *Uttararāmacharita* with Vīrarāghava's commentary: Ed. by

Nārāyaṇa Rāma Āchārya, Nirnaya Sagar Press, Bombay, 10th edition 1949.
22. *Vāmana Purāna*: Ed. by Anandasvarup Gupta, Varanasi, 1967.
23. *Vāyu Purāṇa* : Ānandāśrama, Poona, 1905.
24. *Viṣṇu Purāṇa*: Gītā Press Gorakhpur, Saṃvat 1990.
25. *Yājñavalkyasmṛti* with the *Mitākṣarā* commentary of Vijñāneśvara: Ed. by Nārāyaṇa Rāma Āchārya, Nirnaya Sagar Press, Bombay, 5th edition, 1949.

VI. Modern Studies

1. Agrawal, V.S. : *Art Evidence in Kālidāsa*, Journal of the U.P. Historical Society, Lucknow, Vol. XXII, Parts 1-2, pp. 81-93.
2. Aurobindo, Śrī : *Kāliaāsa*, Arya Sahitya, Calcutta, 1929.
3. Bhave, S.S. : *Kālidāsa*, Baroda, 1964.
4. Chakladar, H.C. : *The Geography of Kālidāsa*, Calcutta, 1963.
5. Chattopadhyaya, K.C. : *The Date of Kālidāsa*, Allahabad University Studies, Vol II (1926), pp. 80-1ı3.
6. Collins, Mark : *Geographical Data of the Raghuvaṃśa and the Daśakumāracharita*, Leipzig, 1907.
7. Dasgupta, S.N. and De, S.K. : *History of Sanskrit Literature*, Vol. I, Calcutta University, Calcutta, 1947.
8. Gawroński, A. : *The Digvijaya of Raghu and Some Connected Problems*, Krakow, 1915.
9. —— : *Studies about the Sanskrit Buddhist Literature*, Krakow, 1919.
10. —— : *Notes on the Saundarananda*, Critical and Explanatory (Second Series), W. Krakowie, 1922.
11. Ghoshal, S.N. : *The Inception of the Sanskrit Drama*, Calcutta, 1977.
12. Gupta, D.K. : *Society and Culture in the Time of Daṇḍin*, Delhi, 1972.
13. Gurner, C.W. : *Notes on the Text of Aśvaghoṣa's Saundarananda*, J.R.A.S. (1928), pp. 131 ff.
14. Hari Chand : *Kālidāsa et l'Art poetique de l'Inde*, Paris, 1917.
15. Hillebrandt, A. : *Kālidāsa*, Breslau, 1921.

16. Hopkins, John : *The Great Epic of India*, New York, 1901.
17. Jhala, G.C. : *Kālidāsa, A Study*, Bombay, 1949.
18. Kalla, Lachhmi Dhar : *The Birth-Place of Kālidāsa*, Delhi University Publication No. 1, Delhi, 1926.
19. Karmarkar, R.D. : *Kālidāsa*, Karnataka University, Dharwar, 1960.
20. Keith, A.B. : *A History of Sanskrit Literature*, Oxford University Press, 1941 (Reprint).
21. —— : *Sanskrit Drama*, Oxford University Press, Oxford, 1924.
22. Konow, Sten : *Das indische Drama*, Berlin, 1920.
    —— : English Translation "*The Indian Drama*" by S. N. Ghoshal, Calcutta, 1969.
23. Krishnamoorthy, K. : *Kālidāsa*, Delhi, 1982.
24. Law, B.C. : *The Geographical Aspect of Kālidāsa's Works*, Calcutta, 1954.
25. —— : *Aśvaghoṣa*, Calcutta, 1946.
26. Lévi, Sylvain : *Le Théatre Indien*, Paris, 1890.
27. Lindenau, M. : Bhāsa-studien, Leipzig, 1918.
28. Lüders, H. : *Die Bruchstücke der buddhistischen Dramen des Aśvaghoṣa*, Berlin, 1911.
29. Macdonell, A.A. : *A History of Sanskrit Literature*, Delhi, 5th edition, 1958.
30. Mainkar, T.G. : *Kālidāsa, his Art and Thought*, Poona, 1962.
31. Max Müller, F. : *A History of Ancient Sanskrit Literature*, Varanasi, 1968 (Reprint).
32. Mirashi, V.V. : *Kālidāsa*, Bombay, 1969.
33. Pusalker, A.D. : *Bhāsa, A Study*, Lahore, 1940.
34. Raghavan, V. : *Vālmīki and Kālidāsa* in KV. Rangaswami Aiyangar Commemoration Volume, Madras, 1940, pp. 409-424.
35. Raja, C. Kunhan : *Kālidāsa*, Andhra University, Waltair, 1956.
36. Ram Gopal : *India of Vedic Kalpasūtras*, Delhi, 1959.
37. —— : *Vaidika Vyākaraṇa* (in 2 Vols.), Delhi, 1965-69.
38. Ruben, Walter : *Kālidāsa*, Berlin, 1957.
39. Ryder, A.W. : *Śakuntalā and Other Writings*, London, 1912.

40. Sabnis, S.A. : *Kālidāsa*, Bombay, 1966.
41. Sankar, K.G. : *The Date of Kālidāsa*, Indian Historical Quarterly, Vol. I (1925), pp. 309-316.
42. Sastri, K.S. Ramaswami : *Kālidāsa*, Śrīrangam (Śrī Vāṇī Vilāsa Press), 1933.
43. Scharpe, A. : *Kālidāsa-Lexicon*, Vol. I, parts I-III, Brugges, 1954-58.
44. Sehgal, S.R. : *Rāṣṭra-Kavi Kālidāsa*, Delhi, 1961.
45. Shekhar, I. : *Sanskrit Drama*, Leiden, 1960.
46. Surya Kanta : *Kālidāsa's Vision of Kumārasambhava*, Delhi, 1963.
47. Tagore, Rabindra Nath : *Śakuntalā* : *Its Inner Meaning* (Introduction to Laurence Binyon's Translation of the *Śākuntala*), Calcutta, 1920.
48. Upadhyaya, B.S. : *India in Kālidāsa*, Delhi, 1968.
49. Wilson, H.H. : *The Theatre of the Hindus*, Calcutta, 955 (reprint).
50. Winternitz, M. : *A History of Indian Literature*, Calcutta University, Calcutta, Vol. I, 1927 ; Vol. II, 1933 ; Vol. III, Fasciculus I, 1959 ; Part I, Delhi, 1963.

INDEX